From Rappahannock County
by
Eugene J. McCarthy

From Rappahannock County
ISBN 1-883477-51-4
Copyright © 2002 Eugene J. McCarthy
All rights reserved
Published by Lone Oak Press
Printed in the United States of America
Block prints © 2002 by Barbara S. Bockman
Photographs © 2002 by Jim Gannon

Introduction

It was near to twenty years ago when Eugene J. McCarthy wrote his first book about Virginia's Rappahannock County, his country home 75 miles and 75 years away from Washington, D.C. He was green back then; the view was a newcomer's. But a few years of early morning discussions at the F.T. Store have seasoned him to local life, where "nothing is quite as simple as it seems."

Finding a "merkle" isn't simple. On occasion the former presidential candidate and senator from Minnesota has found these tasty mushrooms in the woods, but just as often he's resorted to begging for them. He's accepted anonymous gifts. Successful merkle hunting seems to involve blue eyes and the right kind of cap.

Any of these days McCarthy just might master his Lynch's Fool Proof Turkey Call (Model 101). He could virtually hold court at the country story if he managed it. So far he's drawing mostly crows.

These are only a couple of samples from this combined edition of Rappahannock stories, tales, musings and reminiscences by perhaps the last American politician to carry an ounce of poetry in his blood. So lean back, get comfortable and read about a scientific study of roadside trash, fitting chickens with contact lenses and "that treacherous gland, your prostate", about the personalities behind fence types, a proposal for uncle's day and women who assault the comforts of a single man's domain; and why this political man broke his own rule against going to the aid of a columnist in distress. It had something to do with a skunk.

3

CONTENTS

TERRAIN

Rappahannock Revisited

A Second Look

RAPPAHANNOCK COUNTY has not changed very much since I wrote about it in 1984. It is still 75 miles and 75 years away from Washington, D.C. The ruins of old mills still mark the courses of small rivers, runs, and creeks. The number of churches, roughly 50, serving slightly more than 5,000 persons, or souls (one church to 100), is about what it was then. A few church buildings have been given over to other than religious purposes, in a way reborn or reincarnated. Neither word quite applies. In one case, an Episcopal church in Sperryville has been deconsecrated and is now a craft shop, which would seem to be, if a church had to go, a good way to go. The number of post offices at last count is still nine, approximately one for every 500 persons, or one post office for every ten churches. Population growth has been minimal, and the Gross County Product, the local equivalent of the Gross National Product, has been stable, that is, somewhat short of the reported national level. The sub - or secret - economic statistics for the county have never been firmly established. A cursory survey indicates that, as previously, most residents of the county, in the event of a nuclear war would rather see or meet Carrol Jenkins approaching with his pickup truck, chain saw, and other equipment rather than the President of the United States in a helicopter or the Secretary of Defense in an M1 tank.

Reverend Jenks Hobson remains the most trusted clergyman of the county, as attested to by the fact that he still is asked to bless the hounds at the opening of the Fall Hunt. He has been asked why, in the course of his blessing the day before the hunt, which includes the riders, the horses, the hounds and the fox or foxes, he does not include the chickens that are scattered along the prospective route of the ride. Buster Hitt is looked upon as the person most to be trusted if you are interested in used cars, and Junior Baldwin, if you live in the western part of the county, as the best repairman, far superior to Mr. Goodwrench or the Midas man. The groundhog remains the most despised and hated animal in the county, especially by James Kilpatrick, nationally known columnist and a great nature lover, who, it is reported, remains hopeful that a scroll may be found in some high Judean cave establishing that the Biblical curse that mentions thorns and thistles also included groundhogs, thereby giving him scriptural support for his natural case against that animal.

The heavy discussions of national and international problems take place three or four times a week during the lunch period at the Corner Post Restaurant in Flint Hill. More immediate, and possibly more pressing problems are dealt with in the early morning gatherings at the W & J. store on Route 231 beyond Sperryville, a store noted as the "last stop" (depending on what you may be stopping for) before Old Rag Mountain.

Actually, what takes place is not so much a gathering as a kind of moving or fluid discussion in which the participants come and go. In the course of the hour and a half from seven-thirty to nine o'clock, on any morning of the week, participants in the discussions may include woodcutters and wood haulers, horse and mule traders, a rattlesnake hunter, a game warden, a sheriff's deputy, a photographer, orchard men, lawyers, haymakers, and others. The military is represented principally by colonels, although occasionally, in the absence of the established colonels, someone will acknowledge that he was something less than a colonel. The whole proceeding is managed by Wilma Burke who runs the store. Not all stores in Rappahannock County are owned or run by Burkes, but it seems to be better, if one is in the store-keeping profession, to be a Burke or to be married to one. Consumer protection is taken care of at W & J's principally by anticipation of trouble, preventive action. The banana, occasionally offered for sale, is the only fresh fruit ever available and the tomato, the only fresh vegetable. The staple offerings in the fresh or natural order are potatoes and standard onions of good size and not of any of the varieties that are advertised as not causing eyes to water, or as tasting like apples.

The store itself, at least in the morning hours, is a kind of sanctuary. Privacy is respected. Any exaggeration is tolerated and allowed, even encouraged, unless it downgrades the character of some person. There are no limits on what may be told, of war, of coon hounds, of fox hounds or of beagles, of game sightings, and success in hunting. I have reported having seen as many as thirty wild turkeys in a flock, three bears, and three bobcats without noting any raised eyebrows. Reports on mountain lions are more suspect, only one sighting claimed by John Glasker having gone unchallenged. Reports of success in betting on the horses at the Charles Town track are definitely suspect.

The highway department continues its three times a year attacks on roadside wild flowers: the first when the white daisies are in bloom, with supporting blue chicory; the second when the day lilies flourish, and tickseed and yellow daisies; and the third when chicory, wild sunflower, buttonweed and butterfly weed take over. The highway department also disrupts traffic, building three-lane bridges on two-lane roads and leaving the one-lane bridges on two-lane roads. Larry LeHew, the well digger from Front Royal, is still revered for having dug the well that provides just the right volume of water for Washington, the county seat; just enough to meet the needs of thirst and sewage, but not enough to encourage growth or waste. Larry is looked upon as a kind of Moses who brought water out of rock but without subsequently imposing commandments.

Old Rag Mountain

GEOGRAPHY & HISTORY

The Lay & Lore of the Land

RAPPAHANNOCK COUNTY, one might say, is a reborn county; it first came into existence in Colonial times, in 1656, when it was split off from Lancaster Shire. It was named after an Indian tribe and lay in the northern neck of Virginia between the Potomac and the Rappahannock Rivers. The first Rappahannock County lost its identity in 1692 when it was divided into Richmond County and Essex County. In 1749 Essex County produced Culpeper County. In turn Culpeper County was divided by The General Assembly of Virginia in 1833 into Rappahannock County and Culpeper County. This division took place despite the objections of the parent county, which may explain a continuing disposition on the part of Culpeper residents and the Culpeper press to downgrade Rappahannock County and its citizens.

The county lies to the east of the Blue Ridge Mountains. Its boundaries were described well in the original petition for separation from Culpeper County in the 1830s. "Beginning at the corner of Madison and Culpeper Counties upon the top of the Blue Ridge Mountains and running thence with the ridge to the beginning."

One of the strong arguments for separation was that "justice removed by 30 or 40 miles" is likely to be "justice denied."

As it now exists Rappahannock County is roughly diamond shaped with the top point at northwest and the lower point at southeast. To its west and northwest, on the other side of the Blue Ridge, lie Warren County and Page County. To the northeast, across the Rappahannock River, lies Fauquier County; to the southwest across Hugh's River lies Madison County; on the southeast line is Culpeper

County, separated from Rappahannock by neither mountain nor stream, but by a kind of continuing antagonism.

The terrain of the county is rough and broken. It flows down from the great hollows of the Blue Ridge and from lesser hollows and foothills towards the flatter lands of Virginia to the east.

The Rappahannock River, and Hugh's, which flows into it, are fed by small creeks and runs, such as Indian Run, Hittle's Creek, the Jordan River, Blackwater Run, Hunger Run and White's Run, Beaver Dam Run, Rush River and Hazel River, the Thornton, the Covington, and other waterways of lesser importance.

The economic life of the county rests primarily on cattle raising, on hay, and on fruit crops, principally apples, with some support from peaches, nectarines, and of recent development, vineyards. Forest products also make a modest contribution to the economy of the county. Industries that once flourished are largely gone, including apple processing, with major buildings used for such purposes now abandoned or given over to other uses, one, for example, housing the Rappahannock County Co-op, and another providing cover for antique and craft dealers. Milling, a major industry of the county for years, when as many as 70 mills, it is believed, once operated (grist, flour, and saw mills predominating), is gone from the county.

Two service industries, if they can be called such, remain active in the county: one is religion, the other postal service. County records identify nearly 50 churches, either as operating today, or as having been functional parts of the religious culture of the county. Most were and are Baptist, with Methodist and Episcopal churches also running strongly. Quakers, Catholics, and other denominations have minimal representation. The population, slightly over 5,000, is largely of English ancestry. Currently the number of post offices in the county is nine, or one for every six-to seven-hundred persons. The number of offices that have existed comes very close to forty. As in other parts of Virginia, the small county post office has held out strongly in Rappahannock County, in large part because of the efforts of

14

Senator Harry Byrd, Senior, who although he was for efficiency and economy, generally made an exception for the small country offices, which he saw as reminders of government, centers for gathering, and incidentally also politically useful.

While the mills of Rappahannock County ground grist coarse, and the churches ground the spirit exceedingly fine, as God's mills are reputed to do, the post offices refined the politics of the state of Virginia.

Rappahannock County is 75 miles from Washington, D.C., just beyond commuter range, and only marginally within range of Washington's television stations. It does not have cable television, and the number of dishes for picking up satellite programs is small. Moreover, the number of subscribers to the *Washington Post* are few, principally, it seems, because the problem of waste disposal is a difficult one in the county. I cut down my own trips to the trash disposal center from three trips a month to one trip, by canceling my subscription to the *Post* when I found that two-thirds of my trash, by volume, was made up of the newspaper. Subscribers to *The New York Times* are fewer in number than those who subscribe to the *Post.*

Apart from, or in addition to, the fact of geographical protection and cultural insulation, the citizens of Rappahannock County are by nature and history independent. This independence was shown most strongly at the time of the War between the States, when loyalty to the South on the part of Rappahannock was at best marginal. The citizens of the county have maintained this reputation of independence, despite a modest influx of retired military personnel, mostly former colonels, of newspaper persons and media persons, retired, fired, and active, airline pilots and flight attendants and others from the outside. Some proper Virginians refer to Rappahannock County as the Free State of Rappahannock. The county went strongly for Al Smith in 1928, although it had few Catholics and remains today a county without a liquor store, although Smith ran as a "wet."

Ruins of Hand's Grist Mill, Rt. 618

Looking at Rappahannock

Eldon Farm, Woodville

AUTUMN is the main season for looking at Rappahannock County. Rappahannockers look at the rest of the world at any time.

People from the urban areas of Virginia and Maryland, a few other nearby states, and from the District of Columbia are driven or drawn west toward the mountains to look at the change in the color of the leaves of trees and vines as the fall season comes on. There is also some serious looking at Rappahannock County in the spring when the blossoms of wild cherry, redbud and wild plum, followed by crab apple and the glory of the dogwood, give first color to that season, and some casual watching or looking at the county in the summer and in the winter, especially after snowfall or after sleet storms when the winter wonder of New Hampshire and of Vermont comes as well to Rappahannock County. But the truly purposeful looking is that of the autumn.

Most of those who come to look quite probably do not know that it is Rappahannock County they are looking at. They may well miss the sign just east of Amissville on Route 211, but a few miles beyond that town they must, if at all sensitive, note the subtle changes in landscape and in terrain.

Rappahannock land is rougher. There are outcroppings of flint and of granite. The hills are sharper. The road takes on a different character. There are no more of the easy sweeps that mark it on either side of Warrenton. The Blue Ridge Mountains become more blue and Old Rag begins to stand out.

Most hayfields are clear, with the rolled bales fenced in hay lots; and the cows and spring calves graze in pastures and meadows with a quiet intensity, as though they knew they must be ready for winter. The apple trees still carry green leaves. Most have been relieved of their summer's burden but some still show the red and green of late ripeners.

At the roadside and in the hedges a few flowers survive - yellow daisies and chicory, grey-blue asters that have escaped the highway department's last cutting or come back after the mowers passed, a few trumpet flowers blaze among the honeysuckle vines that encumber the fences.

And then the colors begin: first sumac, singed and turning to a savage orange and red; the Pentecostal tongues of gum tree leaves; the dogwood, some green and red and others the color of dried blood. Beyond these are the varied yellows of beech and poplar; of ash and hickory, and elm; the bronze, the copper, and the red of oak trees; and the sudden surprising flares of maples. All these colors are tempered by the remaining green of willows in the low lands and the continuing green of pine, cedar, and of hemlock and of the fir trees that run the ridges of the hills and mountains.

Except in fall the residents of Rappahannock County are scarcely visible. In the spring a traveler passing through the county may see a few of them gardening, feeding cattle, spraying orchards, or loitering on the steps to country stores; and in the summer at the easy and pleasant work of cutting, raking, and baling hay. In the winter, they are scarcely seen, only heard, cutting logs or wood.

But in the autumn they come out. Farmers and their wives and children are there at their roadside stands. The stands - some permanent, some temporary - offer the first and special fruits of the harvest: some late peaches but principally apples in great variety - Virginia Winesaps, Yorks, Staymans,

Delicious, Grimes, Pippins, and others; tomatoes, onions, squash, pumpkins; slightly processed and packaged products - cider and sorghum, honey (cultured and wild), applesauce and preserves - especially strawberry, grape, and peach. Then there are the works of craftsmen: baskets and chairs, furniture and quilts, stuffed animals, and also works of potters, glass, and pewter workers, ironworkers, smiths, and weavers.

In the meadows baled hay is being moved on fork lifts or in wagons, and on the road hay trucks have begun to move. Trucks with wood cut last winter and cured through the summer are headed for the fireplaces of Georgetown, cut and piled according to the measure of a "Georgetown cord." The alert Rappahannock watcher may see the county hunt moving across meadow, field, and hillside pastures, following the uncertain milling hounds or at a gallop when a fox has been raised. Pickup trucks are out in numbers especially on the side roads, some with guns in the rack across the rear window, some with signs of hunting - only in season, one assumes.

Visitors looking at Rappahannock County and its people and its products and wares should know that they are being watched and looked at and studied in turn. Rappahannock County is a good place from which to look. It is backed up against mountains. Most of its people live in hollows, which give security and directed perspective.

Rappahannock County Road

The View from Hawlin Hollow

THE VIEW OF RESIDENTS of Rappahannock County remains much as it always has been. It is the view from a hollow, the best place from which to look out and slightly down on the world, according to my friend John Glasker, an expert on hollows and on looking at things.

The view from the end of a hollow is slightly higher than that of any view from farther down the hollow. But it is not that much higher. It gives the viewer a vantage, but not an advantage, such as he might think he had if looking down on the world from a mountain.

One sees too much from a mountain, says John, more than the eye or the mind can handle. Mountain viewing, he says, encourages careless looking and discourages watching. In a hollow one does both. He watches what is close and small and quick and looks at things that are farther away, with a more general and undirected attention.

Valley viewing also has serious limitations, John says. In the first place, one doesn't quite know whether to look up the valley or down the valley. If he looks up, he may not see what is down. If he looks down, something may move on him from the up side. There is insecurity in valley looking which is not the case in hollow looking.

Looking around in flat land has the same disadvantages as looking from mountain tops or high hills. There are too many directions in which one can or should look. Flat land looking has an added disadvantage which is that one cannot see very far before the horizon closes in.

The view from a hollow starts as at the point of a triangle and widens as it goes out and down. There are some differences among hollows. The best hollow is one that runs or backs up into the Blue Ridge Mountains. Lesser, but acceptable, hollows may be defined by some of the smaller mountains or ridges east of the main ridge.

Among the lesser hollows is Hawlin, where I live. It is formed by the coming together of Juba's Mountain and School House Mountain. It is not comparable, or possibly just barely comparable, according to John, to some of the great hollows just beyond me to the west - such as Old Hollow, Thornton Hollow, Gid Brown Hollow, Willis, Harnes, Swindler, Broad, and several other hollows.

A true hollow should not have a gap but should end with no escape route and with no easy access from its back side. My hollow loses a point on this qualification, since it allows Route 618 to pass between the two mountains, by way of what would be called a gap if the mountains were higher and more substantial as are those which set the limits of Thornton Hollow and the line to Thornton Gap. Despite this weakness, I feel reasonably safe from observation, encroachment, or attack from the rear as I look north-northeast from my house.

With the exception of these two minor faults, Hawlin, according to John Glasker's standards, meets the requirements of a valid hollow and the perspective from it is a true hollow perspective.

A true hollow should mark the beginning of a river, creek, or run. Hawlin does.

It should have had in earlier days at least one mill. Hawlin did. It should have had a school or two and a church. The mills are gone and the schools consolidated.

It should still have wild animals. Mine does: turkeys, deer, a resident bear, groundhogs, transient beavers, foxes, an occasional bobcat (heard in the night and seen twice), skunks, opossum and raccoons.

Every good hollow should have a ghost story or two to go with it, a record of minimal lawlessness, say moonshining, and some poaching and a craftsman or woman or two.

Applying all of these standards, John has approved Hawlin as a hollow and allowed that I may give my address as Hawlin Hollow and claim that I am looking on the passing scene - and even the still scene - with the security, certainty, and desirable perspective of one who lives in a hollow.

Estes Mill, Sperryville

A Tribute to Route 618 (Part of It)

RAPPAHANNOCK COUNTY is secretive and private. It doesn't easily tell much about itself. One must come to know it gradually, a little bit at a time, a small stretch of time, a piece of the land.

I have been concentrating on Route 618 and the land that borders it, and the people that live along it. I have not undertaken to know all of Route 618, not the part of it that runs east of Woodville off Route 522 but roughly the five miles that run west from Woodville to join 522 and 231 in a closing of a triangle.

The first mile out of Woodville is a good road but quite undistinguished. It has a bituminous surface and runs between the well kept fields and pastures of Lane Properties. The fences along both sides of the road are generally free of honeysuckle and sumac and even of dogwood trees. It is an orderly stretch of road that changes quite suddenly soon after the first mile.

The tarred surface ends and gravel and stone take over on Route 607, which disappears straight on, and on 618 which makes a sharp turn to the right. It continues to run between Lane lands, but they become less cultivated and less controlled. To the left of the road is a pasture of sharp hills, rock outcroppings, and patches of trees. To the right, a field suitable for corn and other grain crops; but between the field and the road for most of a half mile runs a band of trees which widens into an oak grove which in turn blends into the woods of Ross Mountain at the next turn, left to the west.

The road, alternately in the sun and in shade, is in winter alternately bare or icy. It works its way around the side of the mountain and, eventually, after crossing two or three rocky stretches, descends to the narrow meadow which marks the beginning of Hawlin Hollow. It is here that 618 takes on its real character and vitality.

At the entrance to the hollow, 618 crosses the bridge over what some maps identify as Beaver Dam Creek - just beyond the site of what was Hand's Grist Mill, a site still marked by the remains of the stone walls of the mill, the mill race and parts of the stone wall of the dam that held water for the mill in what was known as "the big pond." The whole arrangement must have been a masterful piece of hydraulic engineering.

From this point on the road is shaded on the south of a running ridge, known as School House Mountain, and eventually reaches the end of the hollow marked by the gap between School House Mountain and Juba's Mountain, which runs down from the northwest.

There are 11 houses in the hollow, all but two of them still occupied. Just through the gap to the west, on the other side of the two mountains and east of the Hazel River, are three more houses, generally included for social and other purposes as part of the Hawlin Hollow community.

In the hollow there is one working farm, run by Bill and Bill, as they are generally known. It is a highly diversified farm, especially in its animal husbandry activities.

Its livestock includes horses, ponies, an occasional mule, cattle, sheep, goats and hogs, a great variety of domestic fowls such as ducks, geese, guinea hens, and turkeys. There are two partially worked farms, both of which have Belgian draft horses. The other houses shelter persons of various ages, races, occupations and non-occupations, ranging from airplane pilot to photographer, and including one partially retired college professor whose special concern and mission in the hollow is groundhog eradication, not propagation or protection.

The dogs of the hollow include one Greyhound, one Terrier, three Golden Retrievers, one Labrador, a Foxhound, a Beagle of recent memory, one Australian Shepherd and three dogs of uncertain ancestry.

Specimens of nearly all of the small birds of Virginia, including humming birds, live in the hollow or stop by enroute to better quarters, either north or south. Larger ones too come by or stay: vultures and hawks in great variety, including an osprey who pauses during spring and fall migration. Jays and kingfishers and crows are there. The green heron and great blue stop to fish the ponds and streams, and wild geese at least fly over.

A litany of trees can be found along the road in wood lots and on mountain sides: pine, fir, cedar, hemlock, spruce, holly, birch, sycamore, beech, sassafras, gum maple, oak in great variety, hickory, dogwood, cherry, poplar, walnut, crab apple, plum, locust, ash, and elm, and beneath them laurel, blackberry, wild roses, hedge roses and thorn, willows in the low lands, sumac everywhere, and more.

For three seasons there are flowers: wild plum, cherry and redbud, bloodroot, spring violets, wild azaleas, may apples in the spring, anemones, phlox, chicory and daisies, daylilies in the summer, asters, daisies, butterfly weed, ironweed, and thistles in the fall.

In the winter, after an ice storm or windless snowfall, with ice or snow still on the branches of the trees, and the clear black water of Beaver Dam Creek running over the gray rocks between the ice-lined banks beside the road, the scene matches anything that New England can offer.

It is truly a road for all purposes, for flowers, trees, dogs, birds, and other creatures.

An Old Country House

I AM GLAD to have you visit me, but there are a few things that I think you should know about me.

I am a country house, situated with my back against Juba's Mountain, at the end of Hawlin Hollow, in Rappahannock County, Virginia. Juba's Mountain is between me and the winds that blow, sometimes cold, from the northwest. On my south side, I am shaded by School House Mountain, which breaks the heat of the late afternoon summer sun. It also breaks the rays of the winter sun, leaving Route 618, as it passes me to go on through the gap between the two mountains, a precarious, icy road through much of the winter. Country houses are different from each other and very different from city houses, as country mice are different from city mice.

The other parts are quite new, say 15 years old. But taken together, the old and the new, the combination requires some special attention.

The new parts are never wholly free from the old. The new respects the old. The old tolerates the new. The heat is supplied by two old fireplaces and by modern baseboard electric heat. Only the man who lives here understands the proper combination. Do not tamper with the electric controls. Be sure to consult him before you attempt to build fires in the fireplaces. Old boy scouts should be especially careful. The boy scout techniques do not work in either of the fireplaces - not in the one on the ground floor, a very old fireplace, originally built for cooking. It is best to start a fire

25

in this fireplace on the left side of the opening as far into the opening as is possible. Also a window or door to the room must be opened or the fireplace will smoke.

The fireplace on the second floor is different. It was also built 200 years ago, with heating as its primary purpose. In this fireplace the fire should be started on the right side and to the front of the opening. Whoever is doing the firing (I would not advise a first time guest to try), should be most careful in selecting only good dry wood for this fireplace.

I have spoken of the second floor. Actually this second fireplace is on the third floor. The house has in fact five identifiable floors. The ground floor, of two rooms; a second floor, already identified; a third floor for the kitchen and dining room; a fourth floor for another bedroom; and a fifth floor loft bedroom. There are two additional levels. The bathroom and one bedroom can be reached only by going up two steps, and in another by going down two steps. There are three doors in the house which will not give clearance to anyone over five feet eleven inches in height. The seventh step in the main stairway, seventh from the bottom, is three fourths of an inch higher than any other step in the series. There is no problem in descending stairs because of this variation, but people do, unless alert, often fall up stairs. This is disturbing to the person, and also to the dog that lives here.

This dog is a herding dog, of Australian origins. She does not like people who shuffle their feet or who stumble going up stairs. She does not like shrill laughter, sudden changes in voice pitch, or the waving of arms.

There are bathrooms on three different levels. Each operates somewhat differently, the distinguishing factor being the height above the septic tank. On the third floor the use of paper is quite unrestricted. The gravity pull is strong. At the second level, nearer the ground, restraint is recommended, and at the ground level facilities, parsimony.

Restraint is also recommended in the use of water and in the use of the garbage disposer. The water supply comes from a well of limited potential. Showers should be short and scheduled so as not to compete with washing machine loads, dishwasher operations, and other showers.

I am served by a septic tank, not by an urban sewage processing plant backed up by a river or scows that sail out into the Atlantic. Now, a septic tank is one of the wonders of nature, but only if treated properly. Bacteria are its key. Country bacteria evidently do not like orange peelings, or grapefruit skins.

Even though I am well built and sealed, field mice and wood mice do at some seasons of the year make entrances. If you hear a snapping sound in the night, and if you are sensitive to the death of animals, do not be the first into the kitchen in the morning.

Here is some special advice to women.

Do not offer to clean me, or even be caught running a finger surreptitiously along the table edge. Cleaning rules here are lenient.

Do not re-arrange the kitchen cabinets, or offer to do the laundry.

Housekeeping principles followed here are those of England, not of America, a distinction noted by Mr. Dooley who acknowledged that either method - the American using carpet beaters, strong disinfectants, and scrub brushes, or the British employing feather dusters and sprinklings of cologne was good. The choice of methods, he observed, depended on how long one wanted the house to last.

If as a guest, you keep all these things in mind, and if as you are about to depart, the dog jumps into the front seat of your car as soon as the door is opened, you will be invited back.

On the other hand, if you fail to conform to my demands, and especially if the dog nips you or anyone in your family in the ankle just as you are about to step into your car, you may wait long for another invitation. You may not want one.

Rappahannock Weather

THE REAGAN ADMINISTRATION once considered selling parts of the nation's weather service to private companies or possibly even to individual weathermen such as Gordon Barnes or Willard Scott.

The reasons given for the proposed sale were not quite clear. If reducing the national debt were the objective, it would be better to offer for sale all radio and television licenses as new ones are offered or old ones come up for renewal. The offering could be made at auction, in somewhat the same way that the rights to graze cattle and sheep on public lands are offered. The right to graze on the public mind and will could fairly be treated as something the government might also offer to the highest bidder.

The Reagan spokesmen did not say that they thought the private sector could give us better weather or more of it, as they generally assert in their support of the private sector in other services. Competition among weather analysts and forecasters, beginning with ownership of the instruments for studying weather, might give better results than we now get through the competitive interpretation of radio and television weather persons. That competition is not now judged on the basis of whether the weather expert is right or wrong, but on the size of his listening or watching followers. Professional competence does not seem to be a measure of distinction; Willard Scott does as well or better than other weather persons who are "meteorologists." Willard is not.

The early television weather persons were women, like Tippy Stringer. Whereas a few women have held on as weather reporters, they are usually weekend or substitute reporters and none that I know of are "meteorologists." There may be an equal rights issue involved here. In the Old German and Swiss carved weather forecasters, men and women were both included, although there was some discrimination. Usually bad weather, either approaching or continuing, was represented by a scolding woman, armed with a broom, emerging or standing outside the weather house; whereas good weather was represented by a jovial, satisfied man.

The second phase of the Reagan Administration's proposal contemplated the transfer to the private sector of weather analysts and forecasting. It was not indicated whether these analysts would have to be licensed, somewhat as meat inspectors are, or under the authority of the

Consumer Protection Agency or the Environmental Protection Agency or subject to suits for "malpractice" or whether they would have to restrict their terms and measures of weather and its effects to accepted government standards or standards already accepted, although ill defined, with a reasonable margin for error.

Understanding the weather and interpreting the forecasts may become even more difficult than is now the case. One has to distinguish between temperature measurements in Centigrade and Fahrenheit, with the added factor of wind-chill.

One cannot get a simple projection of say an inch of rain for tomorrow, but has to give thought to a twenty percent chance, or a fifty percent chance, that there will be any rain. One must know that "heavy snow" is not necessarily heavy, but likely to be deep, and "light," small in volume. The "discomfort index," a mathematical combination of temperature and humidity readings applicable to government employees in non-air conditioned buildings and triggering their release at a critical point, may not be recognized in the private sector. Air quality indexes and the absoluteness of the pollen count, already under challenge, may be "destabilized" in the new free market weather reading and interpreting. And a new measure, being talked about by the U.S. Weather Bureau, a measure of the stress factor in the weather, may never be tested . . .

All of which may argue for a return of the *Farmers' Almanac* as the best source of weather information, at least, or especially for Rappahannock County.

Cemeteries

Plastic Roses in the Snow

IT CANNOT BE SAID of Rappahannock County, as can be said of the earth, that there are now more persons living on it than have lived on it during all of its previous existence. There are more persons who have lived in Rappahannock County, died, and been buried there than there are in the current population. Cemeteries are given serious attention in the county. Adjacent to most older houses, or marking where such houses once stood, are small cemeteries, some still well maintained, enclosed within stone walls, some with rail fences, and some with wire. Some have been kept free and clear of trees. Some overgrown and marked by thickets of sumac, of locust, of sassafras, or hemlock. A few are marked by ancient oaks and cedars. Of later age and varying condition, are cemeteries adjacent to old churches with graves marked by weather worn limestone markers, some in their leaning defying gravity. Names and dates of birth and death are still legible on some but faded beyond perception on others. In churches still active, at least for burials, granite markers stand among or adjacent to the limestone and marble. Graveyards remain in use, even when churches are closed or gone, like that of the Episcopal Church in Woodville that was destroyed by a tornado years ago and never rebuilt. It seems to be an ecumenical cemetery, possibly accepting the remains of Catholic dead who otherwise might be buried in Culpeper, or in other Catholic burying grounds, or in military cemeteries if they qualify for military burial.

There are community burial grounds, most notably in Flint Hill and Sperryville. Flint Hill bans the placing of plastic flowers, except from November 1 to March 31. Sperryville has no such limitations, and plastic shows on that hillside place in all seasons - plastic roses in the snow of December, unfading daffodils in the autumn, and again, against the green of spring, mixed with flowers brought from garden and from pot. Easter lilies that will stay on unchanged until September, and occasionally the quiet, unchanging peace is marked by a spinning sunflower turning on its wooden stem. Then again late in the year come the plastic roses in the snow to show the men who roll the eighteen-wheelers down Route 522, that someone remembers and is true.

Sperryville Cemetery

Fences

From Robert Frost to Paul Mellon

FENCES COME in great variety of materials, form, and purpose. Good fences may not be quite enough to make good neighbors here, as Robert Frost said they do, or did, in Vermont and in New Hampshire. But bad fences, here, certainly make neighbors unhappy. This is especially true if a bull gets through one to heifers not yet ready to be bred, or an unregistered bull intrudes upon a herd of pure-bred cows.

The most respected fence in the county is stone, full height, standing without help of mortar, unaided by boards, posts, or wire. It tells of hard work in clearing fields of rock, of careful building and rebuilding over many years.

Not far below in rank is the half-stone fence, topped by a rail supported by crossed posts or by a post-supported board or two, possibly fortified by hidden wire and with a strand of barbed wire allowed along the top. These are known as "Middleburg" fences or Mellon or Rockefeller fences.

Next in generic ranking of fences are those of wood; of rails, and boards, and wooden posts. In this class the species ranked first is the worm fence, with oak rails, supported by crossed posts, mainly of oak, not sunk in the ground. These are now largely ornamental or ceremonial marking the lines and limits of old battle fields. A new form of worm fence invented recently by Donnie Keyser, a neighbor, is made of mountain locust rails, laid rail on rail, six deep with crossing ends, and nailed with spikes when not yet dry, six rails in height and sure to last a lifetime.

The most common rail fence, and most used, is the "two post" fence laid in straight lines, with two posts, at measured intervals, bound with wire, sustaining oak rails, some new cut, but most reborn from an earlier fence life. The posts may be of locust, or of treated woods, and the rails aided by a strand or two of barbed wire.

One may see occasionally a fence with rails or poles cut and set in holes in posts, but such fences need not be taken seriously by fence watchers, as usually they enclose no more than grass, and trees, and shrubs, and people.

Board fences are fairly standardized as to material, purpose, and style, with slight variations. They are practical fences, used for yards, small plots, and pens, and pastures. They serve well for horses, and for all breeds of cattle. The posts are usually split locust or treated cedar, the boards of oak, nailed, in orders of three or four to the posts. Some fence builders choose to nail the boards on the inside of the posts, a reasonable choice since cattle push from that side. Others nail the boards on the outside of the posts, and some cover the joined boards with a board running vertically at each post, for strength and also for appearance's sake. Practical fence men say there is no good reason for this way of building fences.

A few board fences, usually of short length, are painted white, but most are treated, sprayed or painted, showing black. Some fencers, cattlemen, not concerned with appearance, but with service, and not raising cattle to outdo the income tax collector, leave both oak and locust unpainted, letting nature have its way.

The third group of fences given place and recognition are of wire, at the lowest level simple barbed wire with as many as four strands, generally frowned upon, except as supplemental to other fences, but tolerated in what may qualify as a temporary fence (not quite as temporary as a single strand electrified fence) around a field in soil bank, or a hayfield, or an orchard for post-season grazing. The wire fence most commonly used by those who practice some form of agriculture or livestock raising or feeding, for a livelihood, if not for profit, is a basic fence of woven wire, topped by one or two strands of barbed wire, sustained by posts of varying kind, with locust or cedar as a rule, sometimes with lesser posts of steel, or spindly locust set between the heavier posts. Such fences are all-purpose. They will hold horses, cows, sheep, and even swine. Some fence builders prefer a narrow roll of woven wire with space below it for one strand of barbed wire, the easier to do battle with honeysuckle, the major enemy of fences in the county.

And then there is the prince of woven wire fences, for horse farms, of the highest order, triangularly woven, guaranteed proof against any horse's folly, and with one board at the top to protect the head and neck of thoroughbreds.

There is one other fence of late introduction, unproved and therefore not generally approved: a high-tension fence, with smooth wire running free in staples or eyes, infrequent solid posts, with spreaders in between, and provision for electric help, to hold disrespectful cows.

Beyond the accepted posts, and strands, and boards and rails, are the fences of the shiftless: a mixed lot, somewhat like the cattle they attempt to hold, parts of old stone fences, or of old rail fences, with interweavings of woven or barbed wire, fastened to whatever is available, downed trees, and standing ones, steel posts, pipes, parts of iron beds. Fences, local experts say, can, if you study them carefully, tell a lot about the character of farm owners, their wives, their economic status (real or desired, improving or declining), major sources of income, kind and value of horses or cattle being pastured, regard or disregard for neighbors, for wildlife, especially for quail, for nature (honeysuckle, trumpet vine, brambles, dogwood, hawthorn, or any combination of the above). A board fence, with faded and flaked paint and some broken boards, usually indicates that the farm or its owner once knew better days. A pasture with economically and socially more acceptable fencing, say rail or board, on the front or road-facing line, and lesser fencing on side or back sides, indicates concern for social acceptance rather than concern for economic realities. Farms with extended board fences enclosing a whole pasture of some size, are usually marked as being supported, directly or indirectly, immediately or remotely, by revenue derived from sources other than the current farming operation, either inheritance or income tax avoidance. Character and social aspirations of wives, too, can be read into quality of fences and into painting and treatment of fencing. Fences broken down and loaded with honeysuckle are usually read as signs of surrender whereas those with hedge roses and brambles may indicate a friendship for quail. Some experts can easily tell, they claim, what kind of cattle the fence was built for (or what kind of horses and sheep). They also distinguish among breeds of cattle, Angus requiring the tightest fence. Nothing in the county is ever quite as simple as it seems.

BIRDS, BEASTS & OTHER GROWING THINGS

Merkles

Merkles

Moments of Truth

FOR EIGHT YEARS, on and off, since moving to Rappahannock County come April, I have been hunting "merkles," the morels of this area. Each season was marked by progressive disappointment and disillusionment with both the merkle and the merkle hunters, until I was very close to giving up on the quest. It was not that I hadn't tried.

I had searched for merkles at random. I had consulted experienced merkle gatherers, following the advice of some who said one should search the south side of ridges, others, the north side, and a few who recommended the west slope or the east, depending on the time of the day. I took the recommendations of those who said one should look near the base of poplar trees, and of those who said the best place for merkle growth was around the stumps of hard pines or in abandoned apple orchards or, as a few advisors suggested, around oak trees.

I accepted gifts of a few merkles, pleading that I or a friend had never tasted them. I elicited promises from merkle hunters that come the next season they would take me with them. Some promised, but until last year no one had fulfilled the promise.

Meanwhile I continued my own efforts using more scientific and more subtle methods. Having heard that blue-eyed persons have more success in finding merkles, I invited my neighbor Dennis Fairbrother to come with me. He has blue eyes. He brought his two-year-old daughter who also has blue eyes. I welcomed her, believing that innocence might be a condition to successful merkle hunting, as it is, or was, in finding the unicorn. He brought with him three brown-eyed Golden Retrievers. I brought my Australian Shepherd, which had one brown eye and one blue eye.

We attended Easter Sunrise Service on Red Oak Mountain preliminary to our search. There were three preachers, each one of whom in his remarks made reference to the certainty of the sunrise, of the coming of spring, of the blossoming of the redbud and of the wild cherry trees, and of other promises of spring that had been fulfilled or would be. I waited for some promise relative to merkles. There was none.

At the post-sunrise service breakfast, half way down Red Oak Mountain, I managed to turn the talk to merkles. Tom Massie responded immediately. I had never looked upon Tom as a merkle expert. I had never seen him wearing the right kind of cap. I knew that he was a fairly good tennis player, especially in mixed doubles, if he had a good partner. He dressed well. I assumed that he was a good horseman, but had never associated him with merkles. I may have been wrong. At the mention of the word merkle, Tom became animated. He told of his successes in finding merkles, reporting that he had once collected half a trashbag of merkles. As he reported his achievements, he turned occasionally to his son for verification. The son said nothing, but seemed to endorse what his father had said. I thought of asking Tom's wife for a supporting statement, but for two reasons did not do so. First, because as a general rule, I never question what merkle hunters say and, second, because of the long-standing rule that a wife cannot be called upon to testify against her husband. Moreover, Tom Massie does, I had noted, have the blue eyes of a true merkle hunter.

I was somewhat indifferent to the approach of the 1987 season. One Saturday early in April (ahead of time, I thought) I saw the usual sign of merkle hunter activity, a pickup truck parked marginally off Route 618, near a mountain ridge reputed to bear merkles. The width of Route 618 is such that one can park only marginally. That was a Saturday; I saw no hunter leaving the hill that day, but on Sunday in a casual walk, I met three searchers returning to their car. They were carrying paper bags, carefully, a sign that they had had some success. I told them, truthfully, that I had a visitor who had never seen merkles, and wondered if they could spare a sample or two. I was given one merkle. This limited generosity was comparable to what had been shown me in previous seasons. I was ready to conclude that all was as it had been in other years. I was wrong...

On the next weekend, on Saturday, in my absence, someone left me not one merkle, but a quart or more, in a sack at my doorway with no identification. This seemed strange behavior. More was to follow. On Sunday I received a call from Tom Massie. My confidence and trust in Tom had begun to fade, but on this Easter day it was restored. He did take me with him into the mountains. The merkles were there in great abundance, as one measures abundance of merkles. I had previously found under instruction a few merkles in old apple orchards, but never before made a true wood's find.

I returned to my house with merkles enough to give to a neighbor, who in earlier years had accompanied me on unsuccessful forays into our woods.

Even more was to come. On the next weekend I received a call from a person in Peola Mills who, remembering my sad story of previous years, recalling my despair of ever finding merkles, wanted to tell me that I was welcome to come pick merkles ("not all," she said) that were growing under a wild crab apple tree, the location of which she offered to give me. I thanked her, and asked to be remembered another year, and reported my satisfying success on the previous weekend, adding that I had even given some merkles away.

I am not yet ready to believe that merkle hunters can always be counted on to be sharing and generous under all circumstances and all seasons, but have revised the judgment that was growing to be almost absolute because of my experience with them in years past, that they were all unreliable - not quite untruthful, but lacking in generosity and a sense of sharing.

My opinion now is that there comes a point at which a merkle hunter who is successful in his hunt is moved to what at least appears to be generosity, both in sharing his knowledge of places where the mushrooms do grow, and beyond that sharing what is found. But that point is not easily defined or predicted. In the dealing with merkles, I believe, a person must reach a point like that of the "critical mass" of nuclear materials, when something drastic happens - explosions, in the case of nuclear mass and "truth and generosity" in the case of the merkle hunter.

Next year's merkle season, I expect, will be different from this one, and from all that have gone before. After observing six merkle seasons carefully and scientifically, and studying the character and habits of merkle hunters, I have concluded that no two merkle seasons are alike, and that no two merkle hunters or gatherers are the same, and even that the same person as a merkle hunter changes from season to season.

From Merkle Hunting to Turkey Calling... & Back

HAVING HAD IN THE SPRING OF 1987, after many such seasons of trying, great success in finding merkles, I relaxed, believing that I had passed the ultimate Rappahannock County test of dedication, concentration, and perseverance and that I could rest on my laurels, or merkles.

It was not to be so. One morning in the country store, I learned that merkle finding was not the ultimate test, but merely the penultimate one and that the real, absolute test for all of the virtues required in the pursuit of merkles is turkey calling. Having had my peace of mind disturbed by this information, I suggested that maybe handling coon hounds might be a more demanding test than either merkle hunting or turkey calling. This suggestion was rejected as in no way comparable, by the local experts.

I had been a casual turkey caller for some ten years, using as my instrument a Lynch's Fool Proof Turkey Call, Model 101, which a friend had given to me. As a rule I worked from the comfort of a lawn chair, and only after I had heard a turkey on Jubal Mountain, which is behind my house, or on Turkey Mountain, a ridge that lies across the road from my house. I thought I got responses, although I never drew a gobbler into the clearing around my house. One February morning, without my calling, some thirty turkeys did come within twenty feet of my bedroom window to feed on the berries of a dogwood tree. I assumed that my summer and autumn calls had had a subliminal effect. My principal doubt about the efficacy of my calls was that often they were answered not by turkeys but by crows.

In any case, I decided to take up the challenge of turkey calling, to talk to local experts and to read what was available on the science or the art of turkey calling.

As a part of my decision I resolved first to concentrate on the call I owned. I reread the instructions on how to use it, and also the claims as to what could be done with it, and set out to master the yelp, cluck, put, whine, and cackle, all of which the box claimed it was capable of producing.

I had a few doubts about my box. First I wondered about why the box was said to be "fool proof." Was it, I wondered, proof against the caller or the callee, the person or the turkey? If the words applied to the latter, it seemed to me that the user of the device was doomed to defeat.

I wondered, too, about the model number 101. Had Lynch tested one hundred models before developing this one, somewhat in the way that the U.S. Air Force had gone through a numbered series of bombers, including those of special note, the B17, the B19, the B52, and finally a B71, after which for some reason the Air Force started over, with the B1 of current use even though it has been crashing too frequently and some experts say that it is not only unsafe but obsolete. It is to be replaced by a new plane, the B2, of the second series of numbers, also known as the "stealth bomber."

Possibly Lynch has a new model on the drawing board (if not in production), a more subtle one. For the immediate use, the Lynch Model 101 seemed to be a reasonably advanced and sophisticated instrument. The sounding box appeared to be oak, a good wood, and the scraper or bow of pine. My confidence in the Lynch call was soon shaken. Again on a Sunday morning, in the country store, I raised what I thought were subtle questions about calling turkeys and turkey calls. I mentioned my Lynch model, only to have a man in a camouflage suit advise me that the 101 was a primitive instrument. He said that he was an experienced turkey hunter. I had some doubts about his claims to being a turkey hunter since he was wearing the camouflage suit. Turkeys, it is generally believed, are color blind and are as alert to a moving camouflaged hunter as they are to one who is wearing red or orange. Some experts hold that wearing the warning colors is likely to save one from being shot for a turkey, especially if one is a good caller. The camouflaged self-described hunter, after asking me to wait, rushed out to his pickup truck to return with what he said was the top of the line in box calls, a veritable Stradivarius. The box, he pointed out to me, was laminated, alternating imported mahogany with native Virginia walnut, with the bow, or scraper, of walnut, to be drawn across the leading box edge of mahogany. My confidence in the Lynch call was shaken, and I began to look about for other calls.

Since I could find nothing in the market comparable to the laminated model I had been shown in the store, I looked to other types of calls. I soon found two calls, the first a variation on the Lynch model, with a sounding board and box of cherry wood, activated by a chalked wooden rod. The sound I was able to draw from this instrument was little different from that which I had been getting from Lynch. My second added call was technically quite different from the other two. It was called "the echo turkey call," the invention of Don Murray of Boston, Virginia. Its central part was a rubber diaphragm, to be inserted into the top of the caller's mouth, and activated according to the following instructions: the user is to put the call on his tongue, about half way back (that is half a tongue) with the rounded side up, and the open end (the call is horseshoe shaped) pointing toward the front teeth. Then he is told to push the device up into the roof of the mouth, hold a little pressure on the rubber center with the tongue, and huff (note well, not puff) from the chest. If the huffed air goes over the top of the call without producing any sound, it may be necessary to trim the tape edges of the call. Evidently this adjustment depends on the shape of the user's mouth. The user is told that he should not expect success unless the seal tape surrounding the diaphragm is tight. The manufacturer makes no recommendation for the use of Polygrip but warns the user to keep the tongue on the rubber diaphragm as he huffs from the chest until some sound is made.

The first sound may well be a squeal or some form of whistle, the user is told. After getting the primal squeal or whistle the huffer should strive to get a continuous shrill sound, and then by dropping the tongue in rhythm with one's huffing, produce the basic turkey call, the "yelp."

This turkey call comes in a plastic container, sealed like photographic film, with advice that the instrument should be kept in a cool, dark place, if not used for long periods of time; that the owner should air dry the diaphragm and then store it in its plastic box, wrapped in aluminum foil, in a refrigerator. Owners are also advised to avoid bending the frame of the diaphragm, and that if they are not completely satisfied, to call or write the inventor and distributor, Don Murray.

The instructions alone were enough to dissuade me even from testing the Echo call, and I gave thought to trying to find another type of turkey call I had learned of, one made from the hollow wing bone of a turkey, and thought of trying the mouthpiece of my clarinet, when I read an article on turkey hunting, calling, and calls in the magazine *Virginia Wildlife*. That article may have saved me from a lifetime of turkey calling. From it I learned that in the opinion of some turkey hunters, calling is much less effective now than it was in the past. The reasons given for the unresponsiveness varied from expert to expert, one holding that calling is less effective because there are more turkey hens available and therefore there is no need for gobbling. Another holds that there are too many hunters and too many turkey callers. One expert holds that the quality and tone of the call is important, another that the sound is all but irrelevant, that what is important is the rhythm of the call. "Every turkey," he holds, "has the same rhythm."

I have decided that until there is more agreement among the experts that I will put off my turkey calling project, and settle, at least for the time being, for the penultimate success, if that is what it is, that goes with successful merkle hunting.

To Beagle or Not to Beagle

I HAVE JUST READ George Huber's sad reflection in the *Culpeper News* on the persistent disregard of Beagles by judges in dog shows, ranging from the Charlottesville show to the dog show of all dog shows, Westminster. According to George the worthy judges in that show have just given the best-of-show award to a Pug. I know very little about Pugs. I have never owned one and therefore, like George, am not prejudiced against them.

George has a Beagle, or Beagles. (I am not clear from his article as to numbers.) I have never owned Beagles. But I did once have a Beagle. Despite that fact I am not prejudiced against Beagles. The fact that I was never able to house train her; the fact that I was seldom able to get her back into the house after letting her out at five o'clock in the morning, the time at which nature seemed to call her, without getting my car out of the garage and patrolling the neighborhood until I found her, often sitting under a tree, waiting, I assumed, for a squirrel that she had treed to return to the ground; the fact that when I gave her to friends because she seemed psychologically unable to stand plane flights, friends who lived near a golf course, she disgraced them and brought them close to exile by persisting in running down every golf ball that came within her range, I did not hold it against her as an individual dog.

The odds are that any other Beagle under the same conditions of life endured by my Beagle would have acted just as she did.

It is in the nature of every Beagle, other things being equal, to look more or less like every other Beagle, and to act just like every other Beagle. This is the nature of Beagles, a result of their breeding, which explains why George Huber's hope that a Beagle may sometime be chosen as best breed at Westminster is a futile hope. It is desperate even to attempt (to a Beagle that is) to be the best of the Beagle breed itself, because ideally the best Beagle is the Beagle that is most like every other Beagle. Not better or worse, not more intelligent nor more stupid. A beagle that is singular, in some way outstanding, violates the principle of Beagle breeding, and consequently is naturally disqualified. A better Beagle might lose interest in rabbits. The best Beagle is the one that comes closest to being an average Beagle. Therefore, every average Beagle is a best Beagle.

Beagles do vary slightly in size and color, but their proportions remain almost the same. It is in their higher faculties of mind that the sameness of Beagles stands out. Beagles are in many respects like a lower order of angels. Experts on angels say that all the angles in one choir are like all other angels in that choir. that all and each are of one mind and of one purpose.

Every member of Cherubim, therefore, is like other Cherubim. They have at all times the same thoughts and the same desires. Every member of the choir of Seraphim is like every other member of the same choir. They all have the same thoughts and purposes, which are different from those of the Cherubim. So it is with Beagles. A beagle that is different, that is "better," would be marked and subject to being cast out or down as Lucifer was when he attempted to be something better or different from the rest of the choir.

This uniformity of mind and spirit in the Beagle is reflected physically in its brain structure. Some years ago the Humane Society, or other friends of animals, discovered that the National Institute of Health was using more Beagles than any other dogs for brain experiments; that the N.I.H. not only was buying Beagles for this use but was in fact raising their own Beagles to supply the needs of their experimenters.

The objection of the friends of the animals was not the experimentation itself, but to what they considered discrimination against Beagles, which it clearly was. The defense of the scientists was that in their search for a standardized brain among higher mammals they had come upon the Beagle brain, and found that, allowing for slight variations, not scientifically important, that every Beagle brain is like every other Beagle brain.

President Lyndon Johnson liked Beagles. He kept two of them at the White House. He said that they (like some Senators) liked to be picked up by the ears.

The Guns of June and July

IN THREE YEARS OF RESIDENCE in Rappahannock County, I found that persons living in the county, and especially those living in the area of Scrabble and Hawlin Hollow, had a deep respect and love for all animals, both domestic and wild.

They were not overly sentimental. They acknowledged the laws of nature, accepting that hawks would prey on field mice and on lesser birds; that foxes would eat moles and rabbits and occasionally, a chicken; that raccoons would eat frogs, birds' eggs, and other things; that skunks had a right to life, along with opossum, chipmunks, and squirrels.

They would use animals against animals in civilized ways: fox hounds to chase the fox, coon hounds to pursue the wily raccoon. They rode horses. They hunted deer, quail, wild turkey - even bears - in season. Poachers were not socially approved.

Among all of these considerate and animal-loving people, three were outstanding: one, a journalist, writer, especially partial to Collies of any size or color but to all other animals, I thought, understanding and friendly. He had written a book about the wonders of animals and maintained the best bird feeders in the county.

The second was a semi-retired professor, a gentle person, a lover of animals. He fed birds and chipmunks, put salt out for deer, maintained oak trees for squirrels and even an old hollow, unsightly basswood tree for bees.

The third was an airplane pilot, sustained in his love of animals by his wife. Together they kept three Golden Retrievers who retrieved only tennis balls and Frisbees. They supported two horses, which they never rode. They had a tom cat, blind in one eye, who spent one third of his time in the veterinary hospital, one third of his time away from home, and one third of his time patrolling the house, holding the mice at bay as his mistress refused to use traps or poison. They had, for a time, four geese. When two of them disappeared just before Christmas and two at Easter time, rather than believe the obvious that the geese had been taken by foxes, leaving no trace of feathers, they accused two of their most trustworthy neighbors of having stolen the geese.

Thus man and nature seemed in perfect harmony, in Hawlin Hollow and Scrabble, until one night at the journalist's house when the talk turned to dogs; I entered the conversation, speaking for my Australian Shepherd. She had not proved herself in handling sheep or cattle, I admitted, but she did have a potent herding instinct and was most gentle with animals, I said.

"Only yesterday evening," I reported innocently, "I heard her barking in the yard. I went out to see her herding a young groundhog very carefully until it climbed into the lower branches of a small magnolia tree. At which point the dog, apparently believing that she had accomplished her mission, abandoned the groundhog in the tree."

I stopped, waiting for approval. None came. There was a pause, then the journalist asked, in what I considered a suspicious tone, "What did you do with the groundhog?"

"Well," I said, "I put the dog in the house, took a broom, poked the animal out of the tree, and chased it off into the woods."

There was a shocked silence. Neighbor looked at neighbor. I was puzzled. I asked myself had I offended someone or someone's dog, or abused a groundhog?

In Minnesota, my home state, groundhogs are of minimal interest and are seldom mentioned excepting as weather prophets on or about February 2nd. I recalled having seen dead groundhogs, tied by their tails, hanging from the branches of trees along country roads in Rappahannock County. I waited in a state of mild apprehension.

The author of the animal-loving book finally broke silence.

"You let the groundhog get away!" he exclaimed. "Why didn't you kill it?"

"I don't have a gun," I responded.

"Then why didn't you use a club? Do you know what you have let loose in this county?" he continued. "That one groundhog in its lifetime can dig enough holes in pastures and in fields to cause ten or fifteen horses to fall and break their legs. Riders will be crippled, possibly killed. That one groundhog and its progeny will destroy hundreds of pounds of garden crops and acres of sweet corn."

"You," he concluded, "had a groundhog treed and let it go, when I spend days lying in wait for one to show up near my garden."

"Groundhogs," he added, and he is a religious man, "should never have been allowed on the Ark."

I left the party early.

The next morning, as I was driving into town to pick up my mail, I approached the house of the college professor. As I neared the house I saw the gentle professor, or so I thought him to be, coming down the road. He was wearing sneakers and socks, shorts and shirt, and a kind of baseball cap, his usual attire for his daily walk. But today he was not walking. He was moving in a stalking crouch, and carrying a rifle.

I slowed to a stop as I reached him. "What's wrong, professor?" I asked.

He looked up at me from his crouched position. His eyes were bright with a light I had never seen in them before. "Groundhog," he hissed. "Keep going."

I went on and got my mail. On my return I stopped to see how the professor was. He had returned from the hunt and was sitting quietly on his front porch drinking lemonade. The strange light had gone out of his eyes. I ventured to ask him about the groundhog. "Dead," he said. "I got him with one shot." He then went on to tell me that in his life time he had killed more than one hundred groundhogs, and that he hoped to increase the number greatly now that he had more time.

Later in that same week, on an afternoon walk, I stopped to visit the airline pilot and his wife. On being admitted to the kitchen, the first thing I noticed was a 30-30 rifle leaning against the kitchen stove.

I had never seen a gun in the house before.

"What's the gun for?" I asked.

"What for?" the pilot responded. "What else but for shooting groundhogs?"

"Your wife won't let you shoot them, will she?" I asked. I had seen her cry when the pigs were slaughtered in the early spring.

"She loads the gun," her husband replied.

I called my gentle dog up from under the table, got safely through the three Golden Retrievers that were guarding the kitchen door, and headed for home.

As I walked down the lane, I could hear behind me the sound of gunfire echoing through the hollow.

Where Have All the Bluebirds Gone? And why?

ACCORDING TO JOYCE KELLY, president of the Defenders of Wildlife, a number of nongame species of birds, including loons, barn owls, wood storks, and bluebirds are "under pressure," and because of loss of habitat and other threats are declining in numbers. My concern for the loons, the barn owls, and the wood storks was immediately stirred. But as to the bluebirds, I had some reservations.

I have tried to help bluebirds. They have been unresponsive to my efforts, spurning a variety of houses that I have offered for their comfort, convenience, and safety.

First I provided a standard bluebird house, built by ornithologist and woodworker Thomas Gheoghan of Scrabble, Virginia. The entrance hole was exactly the right size to let in bluebirds but keep out starlings and other intruders. The hole was placed the prescribed five inches above the floor of the house. The roof was hinged so as to make it easier to remove undesirable tenants such as house sparrows. The house was fixed on the side of a locust tree. It was eight feet from the ground and fastened to the side of the tree that opened on the edge of a meadow. Anti-blacksnake protection was provided. Although the house has been available for three years, no bluebird has moved in.

I offered more sophisticated housing; two houses, in fact, that were given to me by friends, miniature models of the White House, on the assumption that that house is attractive to birds of many kinds. I chose suitable locations for the houses, one atop a fence post and the other in an apple tree.

The house in the apple tree remains unoccupied after two summers. I once saw a wren examine it critically and then leave. Not even a sparrow has deigned to move into it. The other house has drawn the attention of a flicker which set out to remodel it by enlarging the entrance hole. Evidently after getting a look inside, the flicker abandoned the move. Birds may not be political.

Finally, I went modern with a ceramic house, designed by an artist and shaped like a gourd. A wren has moved in and occupied the designer house for two seasons, but the bluebirds, for whom it was designed, have ignored it.

Although I continued to see bluebirds, I took some consolation from reports that the number of bluebirds was significantly reduced. If this was the case, my failure to attract them could be attributed to trends and general conditions rather than personal inadequacy.

The number might be declining because, as the experts were saying, much of their natural habitat was being destroyed by conversion of rural areas into suburban areas. I could understand why any self-respecting species of bird would not tolerate a suburb. But Rappahannock County is not suburban. Starlings might be taking breeding sites away from bluebirds, as some experts said, but there are few starlings in Rappahannock County.

Insecticides, undoubtedly, were having some effect. Yet doubts remained. I continued to see blue flashes along the roads and in fields, and pastures - bluebirds in flight as though trying to fly out of their color.

I began to doubt the experts. Maybe the numbers were not down. Maybe the bluebirds were hiding, or flying so fast they can scarcely be seen or counted. What could be the cause?

I think I have found the answer in Ms. Kelly's report, from which I learned that whereas there were only 15.9 million Americans who hunted wild game in 1985, there were 93 million bird watchers and wildlife photographers loose in the country that same year.

Bird watchers dress strangely and move in unusual ways, not like animals or other human beings. Their hats and caps are especially peculiar. Most of them I know carry field glasses and use cameras. The lenses of all these devices must flash in the sun as they are turned on birds. The cameras click and whir, and some of them flash.

Bluebirds are not secretive, nor are they recluses, but they do like marginal privacy. Ninety-three million bird watchers on the loose may well have driven the bluebirds to more secluded and protected places, where they continue to increase and multiply, I hope.

Neither Love, Nor War

Chicken Neutrality

IT WAS WITH RELIEF that I read a recent scientific report from Virginia Tech. According to the report, Dr. Alvin Leighton, a poultry science professor at that institution, has discovered what seems to be an important fact about the behavior patterns of chickens and turkeys; namely, that longer wave lengths of light, that is, the red and yellow on the light spectrum, stimulate the eyes of chickens and turkeys, and by passing through the eyes, trigger the hypothalamus, which, in turn, sends a message to the pituitary gland to release hormones to begin the reproductive cycle.

The scientist has concluded that if the red and yellow wavelengths, somehow, could be kept from passing through the eyes or reaching them, the hormones that start the reproductive cycle would not be released, and that if these reproductive urges were controlled, reduced in strength, or eliminated altogether, the birds, both male and female, would be more docile, less agitated. The hens in contentment would lay more eggs, and both male and female birds, undisturbed by sexual drives, would eat quietly and utilize feed more efficiently, largely because they would spend less time fighting each other - even to the point that the tendency of chickens, under some circumstances, to peck each other to death would be moderated.

All of these good things, good in the judgment of the scientist (the chickens and roosters, the hen and tom turkeys were not consulted), could be achieved if the chickens and the turkeys were fitted with contact lenses that would screen out the dangerous and stimulating rays.

What is interesting in the report is not so much its potential for increasing the production of chicken and turkey meat and eggs, desirable as these ends may be, but that the report gives scientific support to a method used in handling chickens some 40 years ago. In those days, nearly every farm had a small flock of chickens. Most eggs were fertilized and had to be checked before they were eaten. Chicks were hatched by setting hens, and roosters fought regularly. The most serious problem of handling chickens arose during the winter months when, because of cold weather, it was necessary to house chickens in relatively small coops. In close quarters it was not uncommon for chickens to peck a weak chicken to death. As the Virginia study notes, they may still do so at all seasons of the year.

In those simpler days farmers did the best they could. They thought about the problem and concluded that it was the blood on a chicken, accidentally wounded or struck by a vicious peck by another chicken or rooster, that attracted the flock. Farmers reasoned, or concluded, that if chickens could not see the blood on the wounded bird they would not peck or pick on it. The next step was to seek a way of concealing the blood from the cannibalistic flock. Again the chicken farmers, or at least one of them, thought about the problem and concluded that the thing to do was to paint the windows of the chicken coop red, or rose-colored, so that chickens would see the world through rose- painted glass - or better - to install red or rose-colored glass and put in rose-tinted light bulbs.

The procedure seemed to work despite the word of scientists of the time that chickens were colorblind. It may well be that Professor Leighton has found the answer, and that, although done for the wrong scientific reason, the painting of the window panes and the coloring of the light bulbs, may have accomplished what the rose-tinted contact lenses are designed to do.

Dr. Leighton's findings may have important application to the human beings who, fitted with rose-tinted lenses, may be less irritable, and even less warlike.

Mollie

MY DOG "MOLLIE" spent the best days of her life in
Rappahannock County; irregularly, a few days or a week at a
time between her second and fourth years; and then with a
permanent address, and residence, interrupted by days and
weeks in Washington, D.C. until her death in 1988. It was
here that she learned what ice is, and groundhogs and bees;
met skunks and 'possum, and raccoons; sensed the presence
of bobcat and bear; and practiced her herding skills
whenever given a chance with children or cows. Once kicked

55

by a horse, she gave up on horses; and outsped by rabbits and deer, she ignored them. After one experience with an electric fence, she would enter pastures only through open gates.

She learned respect for cats, but not for dogs, nor for people who laughed too loudly or waved their arms without purpose or shuffled their feet beneath a table.

Mollie was an Australian Shepherd. Australian Shepherds are an unusual breed, first recognized and registered in the United States some thirty years ago. The breed, or what became "the Breed," was brought here from Australia (where it is believed it picked up some "Dingo" blood) by Basque sheepherders. The dog is mainly of Spanish origin, although there is a school of dog experts, a very limited one, that holds that some of the dog's ancestors were Celtic.

In any case, the Australian Shepherd is no ordinary dog. It is, my dog book states, distinguished by "character and intelligence," rather than color, size or conformation. Its eye colors can be blue, brown, hazel, amber, or any combination, with no order of preference. Mollie had one brown eye and one blue one, the combination I prefer. Her ears were as they should be, not pricked or hanging, but broken about three quarters from the base, indicating a restrained alertness. She was "blue merle." Some Australian Shepherds are born with a natural bobtail. Some have to be docked. Mollie, the record states, was docked.

Australian Shepherd owners (that word must be used with qualification, since an Australian Shepherd can never be wholly owned in the way that most other dogs can be, with accompanying obedience, even subservience) are resigned to the difficulties of showing their dogs. The problem exists at the lower levels of canine competition, the level at which the "best of breed" is determined. Every Australian Shepherd, unlike Australian Cattle dogs, or other breeds such as Beagles and Golden Retrievers, is different from every other Australian Shepherd. Each in its own way, therefore, is "best of breed." An Australian Shepherd owner never has to apologize or defensively admit any deficiency in his or her dog. Owners of Golden Retrievers are quick to say, even without challenge, that their dog's nose is a little too long, or that its color is a little off, or that the dog's hind quarters are not quite right, etc. Somehow, by lot possibly, if an Australian Shepherd could get through the barrier within its own breed and be entered in the contest of "best of show," any Australian Shepherd could win.

Meanwhile the Australian Shepherd waits, remaining true to itself - and resisting the corruption of crossbreeding. One sled dog owner thought that by crossing a sled dog with the Australian Shepherd, noted for its intelligence and endurance, he could develop a super sled dog. His experiment did not work. Australian Shepherds are not meant to pull loads. Even when bred down to one quarter Australian Shepherd, the dogs, although they would keep the traces of the harness taut, would not pull.

Their herding quality, the experimenter reported, remained unchanged and when released at the end of a sled run, they would occasionally herd a moose into camp.

MOLLIE

I know that you will not come back,
Not answer to my call or whistle,
Not come even at your pleasure,
As was your way.
Yet, I will leave your "good dog" pad and dish
Beside the kitchen sink, a while,
Your rawhide bone beneath a chair,
The cans of dog food on the shelf,
Your favorite ball,
Hid in the boxwood hedge.
I'll listen in the early morning light,
For your muted huff, not quite a bark,
Suggesting you be let out.
And lie in half-sleep until
I hear your harp-like,
Single scratch upon the screen,
To signal you had answered nature's call,
Made your accustomed rounds,
Checked the limits of the grounds,
For trace of groundhogs, raccoons, even bears,

And now returned intent on sleep
On bed, or rug, or floor,
Depending on your mood.
And if not answered,
Lie down in silent protest
Against my failure to respond
And to show resentment of the
Indifference of the stolid door.
I will not yet remove
The mist of dog hair
From your favorite chair.
Not yet discard the frazzled frisbee
You could catch, making plays,
Going away, like Willie Mays,
But having proved your skill,
Refused to fetch.
Let retrievers tire themselves
In repetitious runs, you seemed to say.
You would run figure eights,
Disdaining simple circles,
Jump hedges just for sport.
Eat holes in woolen blankets
But leave untouched
The silk or satin bindings.
Herd sheep and cattle,
Spurn running rabbits and deer,
That would not play your game.
You swam with ducks
And walked among wild geese,
Ate Tums but not Rolaids.
You knew no dog-like shame.
And died by no dog's disease at end,
But by one that also lays its claim on men.

The Old White Mare

From Borysthenes to Katie

JIM BILL FLETCHER is a well-known, quite possibly the best-known, lawyer in Rappahannock County. He is also known outside the county, in Richmond, Virginia, even as far away as New York.

For years he was the master of the Rappahannock Hunt and in his best years with the Hunt rode a gray (later white) mare, Katie. Katie still lives, nearing 30 years of age.

The poem was written to honor Jim Bill Fletcher at a recent birthday celebration, and turned out better than I had expected, when accidentally or providentially as I was working at it, I read in a history of ancient hunting the story of the Emperor Hadrian's hunting horse, Borysthenes (translate, the Nomad), and of his death and burial as reported on his epitaph.

BORYSTHENES AND KATIE

"Jim Bill will bury that horse," said Clifton Clark
Of Katie, the old white mare.
No one in the country store did dare
Question or challenge Clifton's remark.
"She'll never be trucked to a slaughter house
To be shot, and skinned, and ground into meal,
Or having died a natural death, to a rendering plant,
To be boiled, and melted and distilled
To the essence of horse and beyond.
She'll not be fed to the hounds in the kennel
Or stripped of her hide and left in the pasture
For hogs and vultures and crows.
She'll not be cremated with brush fire and oil
Nor stuffed, moth-proofed and hung on a frame
Like Lee's horse, Traveler, of Civil War fame.
A horse like her is hard to find
And not to be treated as ordinary kind.
She never fell, or threw man, woman, or child.

Yet she set the pace for every ride.
She would jump what other horses refused,
But none but a fool, horse or man,
Would try when she turned aside."
She'll be buried there on the west hillside
Whole of body, with unmarked hide
Not crowded or jammed in a ditch,
But laid on her side in an ample grave,
Neck extended, legs stretched for a joyful run
With Borysthenes, Hadrian's hunter
Who some 2000 years ago, his epitaph states,
"Galloped through plains
And marshy meadows
Past old Etruscan barrows
And chased the Pannonian boars."
"Lived long, and then
With his legs unblemished
Met his fate, appointed,
And in the field was buried."

Trouble in Scrabble

Mephitis Mephitis

Sage and Skunk: Kilpatrick

AS A RULE one should never go to the aid of a columnist in distress. Columnists in trouble should be left, at least, for a few weeks, "turning slowly in the wind," the treatment recommended for his enemies by Richard Nixon or one of his aides.

I am breaking this rule in the case of columnist James, locally known as "Jack" Kilpatrick of Scrabble, Virginia. Jack, as we all know in Rappahannock County, is a noted columnist, commentator, speaker, and writer. He has been an editor. The range of his interests and of his knowledge is extensive. In the course of one week's work, he has been known to give near absolute judgments on problems ranging from how to settle the continuing crisis in the Middle East (one that has been in progress for approximately 4,000 years); and the problem of Northern Ireland, which is itself about 70 years old but is a part of a conflict of much longer duration, approximately the 1,000 years of British interference in the affairs of the Irish; to advise the President on how to control inflation and insure Republican Congressional election victories.

Jack's knowledge is not limited to the world of politics, economics, and social reform. He is an expert also in the realm of nature. He can read storms and seasons. He knows how the moon runs among the branchings of the sun. He can teach weatherlore, and the ways of the wild things. Whereas he is generally sympathetic and humanely disposed to nature's creatures, even those that do harm to his garden and shrubs, he can be hard. He draws the line at groundhogs. If Jack had been consulted in the formulation of the curse put on Adam for his sin, he would surely have suggested, possibly insisted, that to the punishment of the "thorns and thistles" the groundhog should have been added.

Jack has been brought low. If the written word could speak or cry out, there would be crying in the wind in the area adjacent to the Kilpatrick demesne, "White Oak," near Scrabble.

Jack has been brought so low that he is asking the editors of the 450 papers that print his column for help. The profundity of his act of humility can be measured only if one understands that help from editors is the last thing a columnist will accept. In fact the redeeming grace, the distinguishing mark, of a columnist is that he has passed over into that happy state in which he is not subject to editorial review or judgment, either approving or disapproving.

Moreover, having been an editor, Jack Kilpatrick knows how serious it is to ask an editor to stand up from his editor's chair, to come out from behind his editor's desk, to put aside the protection of editorial anonymity, and to speak or write without the covering defense that the views do not "necessarily reflect the opinion of the editors."

What could have brought on this moment of truth? It was a skunk, a female skunk, according to Jack's observation. This female skunk, called Rosebud, has established herself under the Kilpatrick guest cottage and Jack does not know how to get rid of her.

Jack, he admits, has not tried every possible means. Columnists do not have to be pragmatic. They can figure things out through pure speculation. And he has given consideration to riddance methods, ranging from the most violent and primitive means of destruction in keeping with a recommendation in a poem by Yeats for "a bloody and a sudden end," "gunshot, or a noose," to more subtle forms of capital punishment, originally supported by liberal executioners, such as the guillotine, operating on the principle of gravitational pull therefore requiring no commensurate exercise of human strength on the part of the executioner; and poison gas, released by the body heat of the victim. He has even considered inhumane means, either starvation or suffocation by blocking the escape hole with cement blocks.

The more subtle methods of persuasion and of psychology have not been overlooked. Modestly, Jack has suggested that his gardener-caretaker undertake this mission.

Although I have long honored the rule not to tread where angels, editors, and columnists fear to tread, and have hesitated to enter some places where the above mentioned do not fear to tread, the desperation of Jack's call for help has moved me to make one suggestion to him, a suggestion based on boyhood experience on a Minnesota farm long ago.

The whole process was called "twisting a skunk." The instrument: a ball of barbed wire, attached to heavier smooth wire, with a handle (a kind of prototype of the modern Roto-Rooter).

The technique was to insert the ball-end of the instrument into the skunk's den and then slowly rotate it, by twisting at the far end of the wire handle, until the operator sensed some engagement of the barbed wire and the skunk. The compelling principle is that a skunk under challenge or stress will turn tail, but not run from whatever threatens it. The skunk's tail becomes involved in the ball of barbed wire. When fully engaged, that is, the tail and the skunk with its tail immobilized in the wire entanglement, the skunk is slowly drawn from the hole and then disposed of humanely or otherwise.

Whereas, as every columnist knows, and most have said, when in need of a metaphor, a tail wagging a dog is an undesirable relationship; a tail wagging a skunk is the best one can hope for under the circumstances.

Dennis Store, Scrabble

Law & Politics

The Un-Common Law

JURIES AND JUDGES in the county are not quick to find persons guilty. There are no judges generally noted as harsh or hanging judges. Justice is tempered by experience, common sense, history, a sensitivity to extenuating circumstances, such as passion or property rights. Fence lines and right-of-way are given special respect.

It appeared a few years ago that the administration of justice might be a growth industry in the county. That development seems not to have occurred. The threat of growth came from the disposition of two cases each involving use of fire arms and death.

One case involved horse trainers from a nearby county. One trainer was shot and killed, the other did the shooting. The man charged with murder was acquitted on the grounds that his action was a crime of passion. His wife was involved. It was popularly acknowledged, although this was not an open legal consideration in the trial, that the rules between horse trainers are by tradition different from those that apply to the general population.

The second case, one originating in the county, was more complicated. It involved property, a right-of-way, a bulldozer, a pickup truck, a woman in the truck armed with a shotgun, against a man in the bulldozer with a rifle and a revolver. The man was killed, the woman acquitted on grounds that she had acted in self-defense.

These were not typical county cases, which are more likely to be like the recurring one involving Usters Benton Dodson, who has been arrested at irregular intervals over the years for violation of state and possibly federal liquor laws.

Usters is now in jail or out of jail. It is hard to keep up with his record. If he is out, he probably will soon be charged again with the customary charge of selling illegally liquor which was sold to him legally. In his most celebrated arrest, Usters was reported to have had a total stock of two opened fifths of Canadian Mist, which the judge ordered destroyed; 39 gallons of whiskey, presumably bourbon; four gallons of wine; and 38 gallons of beer, all of which the judge ordered handed over to the State of Virginia. The judge also imposed on Usters, who was not in good health, a sentence of 240 days of community service. This penalty was never imposed because, as the county attorney said, there were no community needs in the county that could be served by Usters.

Sperryville Corner Store

The whittlers at the Corner Store in Sperryville agreed that what Usters had been arrested for was probably the best community service he could perform. The whittlers also thought that his arrest was suspect, since the agent who purchased the incriminating liquor had posed as an antique dealer, which is looked upon in the county as a profession, like that of a preacher or minister, which can be trusted and should not be used in scam operations.

If Usters is in jail he may well be involved in the case now pending which is receiving most local attention. This case involves an action by the owner and operator of the Hampton Restaurant against the county sheriff. These are, more or less, the facts or charges in the case. For a number of years, the Hampton Restaurant has been serving meals to the prisoners in the county jail. The sheriff asked that the county return to an earlier practice of having the meals prepared, under the supervision of the sheriff, in the jail itself, the practice before the county entered into the contract with the Hampton Restaurant. The sheriff asserted that he was having both disciplinary problems and health problems with the prisoners because of the quality of the food being served by the Hampton Restaurant, which, basically, he says, is too greasy.

Following the publication of the charges by the sheriff, the owner of the Hampton Restaurant closed the restaurant to the public charging that the sheriff's public statement had driven off her customers. She is seeking damages, but in the meantime continues to cook for the prisoners, possibly including Usters, and to deliver food to the jail.

Several persons have rallied to the support of the Hampton, including one county commissioner who said (he has not yet testified under oath) that he has eaten there several times, without notable reaction. When the case came up, I recalled having eaten there once. (I may have eaten there more than once, but I remember only one stop, some five years ago.) Following a rule of mine which is that when eating in restaurants of unknown quality, it is always, or almost always, best to order "the special." I took that evening's special, which was Swiss steak. I remember the gravy.

To understand the complexity of the Hampton case, one should know something about the restaurants of the county. There are not many, but they cover, with some gaps, the full range of service. At one end of the spectrum, is the Inn at "little" Washington, a restaurant of world class, ranking with the best of Paris, of New York, quite possibly better than any restaurant in Washington, D.C. At the center, the "restaurant of the county," with nothing between it and the Inn, is the Corner Post Restaurant, in Flint Hill. This is the restaurant of the local gentry and ladies, the luncheon meeting place of doctors, lawyers, rural mail carriers, retired government employees, colonels, and others. It is the place where Lions Clubs, Rotarians, environmental societies, and others have their banquets.

Then there are, or were, the fringe restaurants, those that come and go, and others of some stability serving local customers but catching customers in transit. Among these was the Hampton Restaurant, invitingly close to Highway 211, enroute to the Skyline Drive, to Old Rag Mountain, and the Luray Caverns. When I first, and last, ate Swiss steak there, there was minor evidence of decline. The sign, which in daytime read RESTAURANT, at night read only AURANT in neon light. The first four letters did not glow, but a restaurant, appearing to be called AURANT, was not uninviting. The name had a kind of French tone. Then the T burned out. And in the dark it was the AURAN, not a bad name for a restaurant. AURAN rings slightly French and personal.

Next the current failed in the RAN section of the sign, and for several years the Hampton was the AU restaurant and so called by the local observers. Then the U went dark. At the time of closing, because of the sheriff's charges, only the A remained, beckoning the hungry traveler in the dark.

This is the most critical case now pending in the county court since it involves property, the county system of justice, gastronomy, and the current interpretation of punishment, which in some advanced prisons has led to the providing of at least five or six different diets; Kosher, sugar-free for diabetics, meat-free and balanced, vegetarian, special foods for Moslems, and, in one case - this one rejected at a Danbury Prison in Connecticut - a demand for sirloin steak and Bristol crème sherry twice a week, as required by special revelation.

Being forced to eat Hampton Restaurant food, I am sure, will not be ruled as cruel and inhuman treatment. But "Swiss steak" should be banned from all jail and prison menus. The Rappahannock County Jail case may establish a precedent for the nation - unless the widening of Route 211 wipes out the A restaurant and the case.

Miracles on Route 29

Black Birch Becomes Cherry

I MET OVER THE HOLIDAYS a friend who had recently moved from Minnesota to Washington, D.C. He had just gone through his first experience of buying fireplace wood in Georgetown and had found that his experience with wood, its measurement, type, and quality in Minnesota was quite useless in Georgetown.

Having observed the wood trade from both ends of the line - that of a purchaser in Georgetown and, not as a producer, but as an observer of producers in Rappahannock County - I attempted to explain the whole matter to him.

I grew up in a rural community in Minnesota where wood was used for fuel, and I knew from experience, sustained by an education in which measures such as pecks and gills were still taught, that a cord of wood contained 128 cubic feet of wood, allowing for some air spaces, and that the common practice was to measure a cord of wood as four feet by four feet, by eight feet.

My first surprise in buying wood in Georgetown when I moved there, as my friend had, was to discover that though a cord of wood was still four feet high and roughly eight feet in length, in width it was only eighteen inches. I also found that wood was sold as measured in ricks, racks (which in

Minnesota were measures of hay) or cribs (which were measures of corn). The measurement actually depended on the dimensions of the pickup truck from which the wood was delivered. The exact volume of wood in a rick, rack, or crib, I never found out. The sellers did allow a prospective buyer to make a quick judgment by eye and then decide whether the price was right.

Being most certain of the quality of oak wood, and of my ability to judge it, I tried to limit my purchases to oak, but sometimes, under duress - either needing the wood or responding to a seller's plea that I buy the last of his load so that he could get back to the county (Culpeper or Rappahannock) before nightfall or before the predicted snowstorm arrived - I did occasionally buy what was described as a "mixed" cord. A "mixed" cord contained, according to the seller, usually some oak, hickory, cherry, locust, possibly ash, maple, and apple. Sometimes my purchase did have the types of woods listed by the seller. Other times it contained woods that did not fit my recollection of their qualities.

On moving to Rappahannock County, I found that hickory, ash, cherry, apple, locust, and other types of trees that grow there are like the same trees in Minnesota, as are the poplar and black birch. However, somewhere and somehow between the wood cutting and the delivery to Georgetown, something happens to some of these woods. Oak, as a rule, I found, which left the country as oak arrived in Georgetown as oak, although its age might have changed along the way. Wood from dead falls sometimes lost age, and green oak took on age, sometimes arriving "cured."

These changes although noteworthy fall short of the miraculous changes to be observed in the case of poplar that leaves the county (either Culpeper or Rappahannock) as poplar but arrives in Georgetown as ash or hickory. Locust, too, enroute sometimes changes into hickory. Black birch is transmuted into cherry and occasionally into apple wood. These miracles, not unlike the scriptural report of the changing of water into wine, seem to occur on Route 29 somewhere between Warrenton and Gainesville, about half the distance between the rural mill and urban Georgetown.

I gave all of this information to the Minnesotan, and then advised him that the character of the wood supplier was also important. For four or five years I had the same provider in Georgetown. I suspected that some kind of territorial or personal imperative had been established in that part of the city for all other wood men seemed to avoid my house. I got the best wood from my supplier in the early years of our association. When later I complained about a cord I had bought, he advised me that one had to make choices among woods, which, he said, were like women. Some gave heat and some gave light. He went on to give me a dissertation on what kind of wood was best for each variety of romantic situation, and as to which of the senses were most affected by different kinds of wood. He recommended oak and hickory for warmth, locust and pine for sound and color, birch and poplar for light, cherry and apple if it were odor you wanted, or Romance.

As the years of our relationship ran on, the wood man seemed gradually to lose interest in wood and natural phenomena, and to turn to religion. As he became more religious, the quality of his wood declined. As the last wood bought from him smoldered in my fireplace, I read the card he had left. It encouraged me to have faith in the Lord and in my fellow men (including wood sellers), and advised me to "Keep Smiling."

I advised the Minnesotan, first, to buy only oak and, second, to settle for a "Georgetown Cord" over ricks, racks, cribs and other odd measures and, third, to be careful of philosophical wood sellers and, fourth, to shun those who offered religion, especially with mixed wood.

PUBLIC & GREAT AFFAIRS

Computers Haven't Found Rappahannock Yet

THE STORY of how a pair of youthful computer experts broke into the Los Alamos National Laboratory computer (which by report contains sensitive defense information) and continuing stories of how money or title to it and information of sensitive and personal character is being illegally or extra-legally taken from computers have stirred a rash of commentary.

Some commentators are relieved to know that it is possible to find out what the government is up to, whether in the field of nuclear arms or in its handling of citizens' affairs. Others, who favor more government security, are disturbed. Some observers argue that there should be more control over the use of computers; others say that the computer is innocent and that the problem is basically a human one.

Some analysts of social behavior and guardians of the common good say that the kids who broke into the major computer systems should be punished as an example. But at least one such guardian says that they should be rewarded for demonstrating that the people can watch the watchers and find out what the government or big business and financial institutions know about the people. Joseph Weizenbaum, of the Massachusetts Institute of Technology, has contributed the philosophical comment that "there is no such thing as absolute safety," not in or outside the computers.

He is right. But if one looks for relative security and privacy, or for what is left of either, there is evidence that both are still to be found and enjoyed in Rappahannock County. It is not likely that a computer will embezzle money, for example, from the Rappahannock National Bank. The telephone lines here are reasonably secure and even the integrity of party lines is high. More important than these evidences of local security of property and person is the evidence that the big national, possibly even international, computers have not quite discovered or defined life in this county. I cite two recent examples that are reassuring.

A few months ago I received a very enticing offer from the *Reader's Digest.* I have forgotten all of the details of the offer, but basically, a whole field of possibilities were opened up to me in return for an initial six months' subscription to the magazine. My early indifference seemed to irritate the *Digest* computer which, following my failure to respond to the first shining offer, chided me for my insensitivity. I was beginning to feel some guilt when there arrived through the mail another ultimate offer, or promise, or enticement, which was that if I hurried and did what the *Digest* computer wanted me to do, I might somehow come to own a "second house" in Woodville, Virginia. I concluded that Woodville was not fully understood by the *Digest* computer.

Having hardened my resolve against the *Digest* appeals, even the prospect of that second home in Woodville, I was struck by another computerized appeal. This one came from the Smithsonian Institution, which opened its communication with this disarming note, "I know you receive many personal (i.e., computer printed) invitations, but this is special."

The letter assured me that I was "one of a small group" of Woodville Residents (capitalized) invited to become National Associates of that prestigious Institution.

I have not checked with the boys who sit on the post office stoop each morning, waiting for the mail to be distributed, to see which of them is included in the small group that has been favored and identified by the Smithsonian computer, but will do so next Monday.

U.S. Post Office, Woodville, Virginia

Of Arms, Chess, and Poker

AFTER YEARS OF TRYING, I have figured out why the Russians and the Americans could make no progress in negotiating a limit on nuclear arms buildup, even after both sides had, according to authorities, sufficient nuclear military power to destroy each other ten or twenty times. It was marginally within reason to allow for two destructions, in fear of second comings, and possibly on the suspicion that Russians, like cats, might have nine lives; but to go beyond these limits was to move into the range of unreason.

Discussions of arms control and limitations began in the Eisenhower Administration and have continued in fits and starts (more have been started than have been concluded) through five succeeding presidential administrations and on into the Reagan period.

As each new weapon system, missile, bomb, submarine, airplane, etc. was proposed, it was almost inevitably described by its U.S. advocates as a "bargaining chip" which would surely improve our position at the bargaining table. Thus the Reagan Administration has stated that the MX missile, even if placed in a vulnerable silo (possibly particularly so), would be a bargaining chip. Obviously, a bargaining chip must be exposed. It is not like a card held in a poker hand which has not been shown to one's opponents at the table. The administration does not say whether it considers the MX as a "white chip" for openers; as a "red chip" for a possible deterrent; or as the final, heavy offering, a "blue chip."

Former Vice-President Mondale questioned the effectiveness of the MX as a "bargaining chip." He did not say why, nor did he oppose the use of bargaining chips. He said that if we want bargaining chips, there are plenty available.

The difficulty in all of these negotiations is one of language, of metaphor. The Russians are not heavy into poker. In fact, I know of no Russian poker players. Their game is chess. Their images in international negotiations must certainly be drawn from their game.

Chess is an orderly game, a defined one. It is played on a board. Each piece has a special value. Its moves are prescribed. Although chess allows for a "ploy," it has little room for bluffing. There are no hidden cards and the game ends because certain conditions are met, not as in poker because participants run out of money or because they are exhausted.

In keeping with this analysis, it is understandable that the Russians could agree to SALT II, which provided for an end to the game when certain conditions were met in "checkmate" in the year 2000. The concept of checkmate is foreign to the thought of poker players. Poker does not allow for ties. George Kennan in an analysis of the Helsinki Agreement points out that it was consistent and in character for the Russians to agree to the territorial provisions of that Agreement, which were specific and defined; but it was folly to believe that they understood or accepted the human rights provisions of that Agreement as we did.

Russians and Americans should, before undertaking further disarmament discussions, agree on common imagery. Possibly one meeting could be held in which all figures of speech had to be drawn from poker and another from chess. There would still be room for negotiation and misunderstanding, but some of the difficulties might be overcome. The vulnerable MX, instead of a "bargaining chip" could be considered as a "pawn" in chess.

The B-1 and the Russian Backfire Bombers would be deemed as knights, our aircraft carriers as "bishops" moving only on the diagonal, to be matched by Russian tanks, also considered as "bishops" although operating on land rather than on water. The anti-ballistic missile instruments and technology could be considered as "castles;" our nuclear submarines and those of the Russians as "queens," the most dangerous striking forces. Conventional weapons on both sides, unless the nod goes to heavy, exposed missiles, might serve as "kings," the last to be called into play and the last to go.

It was the unanimous opinion of the participants in Harvey's Saturday night poker game in Woodville that negotiation in the language of chess should continue but that Russian diplomats should be asked to take up poker and American diplomats should learn chess. Then when agreement was reached in the language of both games, that agreement should be sealed and accepted by both parties.

Rules, Rules, Rules

HAVING NOTED, under protest, the refinement and censorship of language and actions of baseball players, coaches, and managers in reaction to umpires' decisions, I was challenged to understand the new professional football rules designed, I was informed, to protect players and also to make the game more exciting by giving new advantages to the offense.

National Football League scores are now reaching the level of basketball game scores of the 1940s and 50s. The football rules are something else. There are zones within which players are allowed to bump other players, and zones in which they may not.

Under some circumstances players may be bumped only once; under others they may be bumped twice, but not by the same players. (I think this is right.) In some zones blocking above the waist, or the belt (a more manly term, since the waist was first identified in the corset age), is permitted, but only from the front. Blocking above the waist from the back, in these zones, is not allowed. Blocking below the knees, from the front, is permitted in some zones and not in others, whereas blocking below the knees from the back is generally forbidden, excepting in a very narrow zone.

Face-masking is generally forbidden and punishable by penalty, although a distinction is made between intentional and unintentional face-masking. Just how the referees, in an instant, can determine the intent of the face-masker, I have never been told. Television sports commentators seem to know, and are able to tell the audience immediately.

My proposal for the face-mask problem is to use barbed wire, or else to electrify the wires or bars and the face guard, so that violators would be deterred, either by barbs or by shocks. Gang tackling may soon be forbidden, and superseded by a touch-football tag, which could be enough to stop a wide receiver after he has made a catch. It has been suggested that on punt returns the receivers not be protected by blockers, but be given something like a 10-yard running start before they can be touched, spoken to or looked at with anything but kindly eyes.

All of these disturbing sports developments pale into insignificance and irrelevancy when set against a new proposal coming out of the Atlantic Coast Conference. Officials in that league have been instructed by the league office to crack down on violations of "bench decorum" rules. There is a feeling, the league office reports, that not enough technical fouls were called last season.

At the same time as this recommendation was made public there was another report that the incidence of heart attack among basketball coaches was well above the national average, and above the level of such attacks among coaches in other sports.

Basketball coaches are to be restrained, the Atlantic Coast Conference is proposing, forced to remain sitting, unless rising to give a signal. "Instantaneous and/or spontaneous reaction by players to an outstanding play is acceptable." Note the reaction must be instantaneous but it need not be spontaneous. It can be spontaneous, that is, without reflection, but possibly, slightly delayed. This reaction is allowed to players, and not to coaches. Coaches are expected to be under control, and especially assistant coaches, who, the ACC office suggests, are the worst offenders.

The crowd, too, may have to be regulated, its cheers modulated so as not to arouse passionate responses. Any banner reflecting racial, religious, political, historical, personal prejudice or even differences, may have to be removed from the gymnasium. If ACC's proposals prevail, cheerleaders may have to be modestly dressed and restrained in their gymnastic and physical appeals to the crowd, and coaches will be tied to their chairs, until carried away to the asylum or the cardiac ward.

Days of June, 1981

What is so rare as a day in June
Then if ever come perfect days
Then heaven tries earth if it be in tune.

So wrote the poet, and so I accepted his word for this June, expecting that I would have to contend with minor physical discomforts, all products of nature in the process of reproduction and growth: a barn swallow that has taken to nesting in my garage, forcing me to cover my car, especially after her eggs have hatched and the fledglings have taken to eating solid food; a swarm of bees that had to be discouraged after they had established their hive in the walls of my attic; assorted minor allergies; various blights and bugs that attack flowers and garden plants.

June was going well, close to the poet's description; and then I realized that as the month went on almost daily there were arriving through the mails progressively disturbing messages.

June was, I was reminded, no time for complacency; no time for quiet communing with nature; no time for political indifference, even though there would be no Congressional elections until 1982 and no presidential election until 1984. It was later than I thought, was the prevailing message.

First was the League of Women Voters, telling me that I needed its help and protection against folly and partisanship, even bi-partisanship. This puzzled me some since in 1976 the League had taken a strong position in favor of strengthening and preserving the two-party system, as they called it. Evidently something had happened that I had missed in the years since 1976.

Then came a request for support from Americans for Democratic Action, to stand against reaction and to play the cards still left from the New Deal.

A relatively new organization called "People for the American Way" was the next to disturb my quiet reflections: in the daylight, among bees and butterflies, and some lesser insects, and in the evening as I watched fireflies against the woods, listened to frogs and tree toads, and inhaled the nighttime scents, including honeysuckle (the last, a reminder that the curse of Adam still runs). "People for the American Way" has been organized by Norman Lear, a good man of television fame. Its purpose is to protect me from the loss of freedom of thought, religion, and speech, two of which freedoms I have all but lost to television, yet no one of which seemed particularly threatened at the end of Hawlin Hollow where television reception is very bad and there is little religion and few people to talk to.

A warning from Common Cause was next to arrive. The threat, it seems, is "private interest" and "special interests." These will be contained, if not driven off, by Common Cause - the only, self-designated, "public interest" lobby in good standing. The Common Cause appeal is attractive. It does not ask me to do volunteer work, nor to maintain any anxiety. I can relax. Common Cause will worry for me and watch in the daylight for the "noon-day" devils and after dark for "the evils that move in the night." All I need to do is send money.

Since I was experiencing no disturbing noontime anxieties and no disturbances in the night, I put this appeal aside only to be challenged the next day by another call to concern, this time by an organization named "Americans for Common Sense," recently founded by former Senator George McGovern. The danger to the Republic, as seen by these Americans, is from irrationality, from the radical right, and from the new members of the Senate who are judged to have brought "visibly less creativity, vision, and talent to the service of the nation than was brought to it by former Senators." As a former Senator, I am inclined to agree, although I find it hard to imagine how one could determine that the new crop had "visibly" less vision unless one were an ophthalmologist, or possibly an optometrist.

The appeal and warning of "The National Committee for an Effective Congress" came next asking me to help keep the House of Representatives free from control by the "right wing," which now, according to LACED, controls the White House, the Senate, and the Supreme Court.

Only one appeal arrived in June from what might be called a "right wing" group. "Young America's Foundation" wrote asking me for help in their effort to counter Marxist propaganda on our college campuses. I had been led to believe that the problem with college students was not Marxism, but something called "apathy."

I have been pondering on the reason for this flood of requests, strongly weighted on the liberal side. Liberals, I have concluded, are more worried in the spring and summer about the uncertainties of the growing season. Conservatives, whose appeals multiply in the fall and winter, are worried about preserving the harvest.

I think I will get out my Lynch's "fool proof turkey call" and try my skill on the gobbler that moves daily across the ridge of Turkey Mountain.

4ᵗʰ of July - Rappahannock Reflections

I WAS RECENTLY ASKED to write a Fourth of July essay to go with what was billed as "an old-fashioned Fourth of July." As it turned out, the Rappahannock County observation of the nation's birthday in Washington, Virginia, the county seat, was not "old-fashioned" except that it was in the continuing tradition of the Day.

The Fourth of July is properly called a "Celebration." It is not a day dedicated to recollections of national greatness, of tragedy or of success. It is not a day on which a great historical military victory was won.

The first Fourth of July was a day of dangerous commitment. It was a day of uncertainty and also of faith. A day of fear, but of hope as well.

On that day, July 4, 1776, Congressional representatives of the thirteen American colonies assembled in Philadelphia to declare independence from England of the thirteen American colonies.

They based their declaration upon the asserted right of all men as created equal and endowed with certain inalienable rights, including life, liberty, and the pursuit of happiness.

This was their belief, of which G. K. Chesterton in a book called *What I Saw in America* wrote after he had visited this country in 1922: "America is the only nation in the world that is founded on a creed. That creed is set forth with dogmatic theological lucidity in the Declaration of Independence; perhaps the only piece of practical politics which is also theoretical politics and also great literature."

The ideas that were incorporated in that document did not come out of a think tank or a problem solving session, but were gathered and refined from the history of self-government and from reflection on theories of government and social organization.

The men who drafted the Declaration, principally Thomas Jefferson, and those whose thought sustained the Revolution, were not alone in their own time. With them were men who had studied liberty in the past, and who had looked to government as an instrument for attaining and securing that liberty.

Plutarch was there, and Plato and Aristotle. Machiavelli was a consultant. Political philosophers like Rousseau, Montesquieu and Locke were known and present in their writings.

But the heroic act, both in spirit and physically, was that of the men who signed the Declaration, who pledged their "lives, their fortunes, their sacred honor." If the revolution failed, they were not destined to the simple disappointment of political defeat. There was to be no easy retreat to the farm, or to their businesses, or professions, as is the case with defeated politicians in our day.

Their fortunes were forfeit, and their lives, by gunfire or hanging; and one can anticipate, since history would have been written by victors, their honor was denied.

The goals set for this new political society were uniquely different from those set in most documents asserting revolutionary goals. They were "life, liberty, and the pursuit of happiness," not as separable goals, but as a trinity, interdependent and mutually sustaining and continuing.

There was no promise or projection of completeness and absolute fulfillment, but rather a challenge to continuing effort and struggle. Life was promised, but within the context of liberty, a word which encompasses freedom and restraint.

The Declaration did not project society such as that which the cry of the French Revolution offered, one of "Liberty, Equality, and Fraternity."

It did not project a society of defined order, and of complete satisfaction, but one in which men and women could "pursue happiness," something not offered as a goal in any other political document, declaration, or constitution before or since the Declaration of Independence was signed.

Unlike the French Revolution which promised a society marked by fraternity, the American Declaration took fraternity and brotherhood as a prerequisite and continuing base for political change.

The Declaration did not promise happiness, something either so obvious or so personal as to have little meaning in a public document, but conditions in which all could "pursue happiness."

The word "happiness" as used in 1776 was of somewhat different meaning from that which is given to it by song writers and advertising copy writers in our own time. It was not the brand name for a vague, passive "happy hour" kind of existence, but rather a state of satisfaction in effort and in achievement as used by John Adams who, in writing of the Revolution, said that it was won before it was fought.

For there was present, he said, among the colonists, the "spirit of public happiness" which included delight and satisfaction in taking part in the execution of those decisions.

It is in this spirit, continuing, unchanging, that the Fourth of July has been celebrated through the past and in the present. It is a living celebration with no break between past and present, even in its rituals of flags, parades, food, mingling of religion and politics, of church and state without court challenge, old and young, music and noise, shouting and quiet talk and patterned political speeches, sobriety and some drinking.

Reports of the earliest Fourth of July celebrations are little different from those held every year in Washington, Virginia. A Fourth of July celebration always seems to have an element of uncertainty, some risk, a little more than has been planned or anticipated. It is a kind of happening, an existential experience, which it was before existentialism was identified.

My earliest recollections of Fourth of July celebrations include decorated floats, generally hayracks drawn by horses, the pride of their owners, with the risk of an occasional runaway. The booths in the park, serving food, were usually run by the churches.

Each church, Methodist, Baptist, Anglican, Lutheran, and Catholic, over the years developed its own reputation as a food provider and its specialties, not, in some cases, unlike their theological differences.

The first respectable exposure to gambling (the Revolution was a gamble) were throwing balls at pyramided milk bottles; tossing rings for canes; bingo; and more serious games with real money and spinning wheels that small boys were permitted to look at, but not play.

The noisemakers of the day were explosives, some marginally illegal, beyond the size of the firecracker called "Minnesota Limits," the maximum power allowed by law. They were supported by cherry bombs, Chinese firecrackers, and "snakes" - all conditioned by the smell of punk. Finally came the evening magic of fireworks - sparklers, roman candles, rockets - sometimes staged by professionals, sometimes staged by the local volunteer fire departments whose members were reputed to be expert in handling fire.

I remember listening to the band music and later playing in the bands. I remember the baseball game, antecedent of the modern major league all-star game since small town teams (which in league play had to go with local talent) could for the Fourth hire outside talent, say a pitcher from Minneapolis.

And then the political speeches, usually given by a local politician but occasionally by someone of state-wide reputation and even national fame. The one I best remember was given by Magnus Johnson, a man of strong and clear Scandinavian descent and of even stronger Scandinavian accent. He was for a time the U.S. Senator from Minnesota.

His closing speech lines usually were "I look like a farmer. I talk like a farmer. I act like a farmer. And, by heck, I am a farmer." To which he added on the Fourth of July, "And, by heck, I am an American."

Which is what every American can and should say with modesty, with dedication, and with pride on the day described by George Washington Plunkett, a political boss of the Tammany organization in New York at the turn of the century as "that glorious day."

Ultimate Defense of Rappahannock County

JUST BACK from an unsuccessful 1982 Senate campaign in Minnesota, I felt obligated to report that I did my best to defend the county and its residents under attack from press and politicians.

The fact that I had been born in Minnesota and had served the state twenty-two years in the Congress of the United States was dismissed by my Minnesota detractors as a minor qualification. My proposals for dealing with the crisis in housing finance were discounted. My program for the orderly marketing of agricultural products in international trade, without ill-advised and ill-timed interventions by Presidents and Secretaries of State and by Congress, was set aside as irrelevant, as was a defense tax recommendation which would have equalized American competition with Japanese and German manufacturers and helped finance the federal debt. My plan to schedule a reduction in the arsenal of nuclear weapons was not weighed seriously.

The central, almost the sole issue of the campaign, was that I had been living, as my critics said, "down" in Virginia, in "Rappahannock County," with Virginia gentlefolk for twelve years.

In my defense I pointed out that I had been living in the county for only five years, and that consequently whatever baneful effect life in the county might have had on me was limited to five years, rather than twelve; and that by quantitative measure, depending on how the percentages were figured, my critics were either 120 percent wrong, approximately, or approximately 70 percent right, both errors being well within the tolerable margin of error in political campaigns.

Having challenged the arithmetic of my critics, without noticeable effect, I turned to their history and geography, noting, first, that if one is living in Rappahannock County, he is not living "down" in Virginia, but "out" in Virginia; that Rappahannock County is commonly referred to by established Virginians as the "free state of Rappahannock" and that some residents of the county were not above suspicion as to their loyalty to the South during the Civil War or, as it is called in Virginia, "The War between the States."

These responses seemed to stop the critics momentarily but they came on strongly, charging me with "associating with Virginia gentry in Rappahannock County." This was a difficult issue for me and one that got me into deep trouble. I said, in fact asserted, that there certainly were a good number of ladies in Rappahannock County but that the number of men of my acquaintance who could properly be called "gentlemen" was small, and that even though the sports and games - fox hunting, point to point racing, even some polo playing - were by definition and tradition the sports and games of gentlemen, if not of kings, and though the participants were properly dressed, they were not necessarily gentlemen, of the quality of those engaged in similar activities, say in Warrenton, Upperville or Middleburg, to name a few places that might be recognized by what is called the "horsey set" in Minnesota who ride to hounds but not to the fox. Rather they follow a drag across well-trimmed field, over custom-made fences, walls, and hurdles. Real foxes, in any case, are hard to find in Minnesota, and if found are not to be hunted or chased - not on horses, not on motorcycles, or in snowmobiles.

To further distinguish Rappahannock County riders from those of other parts of Virginia, I pointed out that for a variety of reasons - roughness of terrain, boldness of riders, frequency of groundhog holes, and other things - many gentleman and lady riders from other Virginia hunts were hesitant to ride with the Rappahannock riders.

The case was not allowed to lie at rest. I was challenged to explain who, if not gentlemen, lived in Rappahannock County. I acknowledged that there were one or two gentlemen in the county and another two or three marginal ones, whose names I refused to give out, and went on to explain that the men of my acquaintance in the county were country lawyers, well diggers, preachers, horse trainers and traders, orchard men, cattle breeders and horse breeders, wood cutters, timber men, a game warden, at least three country store owners, an auctioneer, two filling station operators, the keeper of the hounds, a real estate man who encouraged people to eat rutabagas, a county supervisor, one or two persons suspected of being moonshiners and bootleggers, poachers, a coon hound trainer and hunter, and one suspected of keeping fighting chickens, and a few scattered United Airlines pilots.

Finally sensing that my list was not impressing my critics, I threw in the names of several retired newspaper and television persons, and the name of Jack Kilpatrick, hoping that I might be saved by that conservative association.

It was all to no avail but the integrity of Rappahannock County survived unscathed. My ultimate explanation was that Virginia as a state is known as the mother of Presidents, whereas Minnesota is getting a name as the mother of Vice-Presidents, at least for the Democratic Party.

PEOPLE

John Glasker: The Handy Man

JOHN GLASKER was a true "handy man." He considered himself a painter, but that was just for openers. His skills were many, and of varying degrees of mastery. As painter he specialized in painting or re-painting metal roofs on houses and barns, both difficult and dangerous tasks, and solitary. John preferred more social jobs, allowing for conversation and commentary and community spirit. What he sacrificed in painting, he made up for in other jobs he performed.

John, as a treeman, could cut down trees, trim them, cut them into manageable lengths or blocks, and split the blocks. Each tree John cut was thoroughly discussed before it was operated on, much in the way in which a surgeon analyzes a patient before operating. The type of tree was considered, its size, and location. Trees growing on a side-hill were to be handled differently from those growing on the flat. Trees growing on a north slope differently from those growing on a south slope. After a becoming pause during which the parties to the action discussed the mastery of the felling, John moved with the chain saw to the central action, of trimming the tree of its branches and cutting it into manageable lengths, a veritable ritualistic dance.

All of this was accompanied by a running exposition of the relative merits of oak, hickory, black birch, and other types of trees, as sources of heat, light, sound, and odor.

The second specialty on John's list of skills and services was that of killing and butchering hogs, an operation which involved science, tradition, myth, and experience, all relative to the act of transforming a hog into pork, thus accomplishing a fulfillment of the pig's life in its death. The arrangements were meticulous. The pit for the fire to heat the water for the scalding, not too deep or too shallow, but just right to allow draft, while retaining and concentrating heat on the scalding tub.

The tripod of locust poles had to be set right, with the pulley in place for the lifting and hanging of the carcass. The general temperature, a Thanksgiving Day one, just about freezing. The presence of blue-bottle or green bodied flies indicated that the temperature was too high, a critical point in the process, as was that of the water in the scalding tub, which John said could be determined, without scientific or instrumental help, only by testing with fingers and thumb.

At the proper moment John would signal the beginning of the process of scraping off the bristles. Commercial scrapers were tolerably useful, but John preferred the top of home-canning glass jars. John, handily, was also a master of pig-roasting, if the need arose.

~~~

John was, as I see him now, a kind of transition man. He changed trees into wood and lumber and rails: Pigs into pork. And in his third special field of competence, grass into hay and mulch and into lawns. He could use mowers and weed-eaters, but he really came into his own when the job called for, or permitted, the use of a scythe. John's first act was to sharpen his tool. Sharpening his scythe, preliminary to beginning the cutting, and repeated as necessary during the continuation of the work, was no ordinary process, no routine running of the whetstone up one side of the blade and then up or down the other. The sharpening was done to a syncopated rhythmic beat of John's own making. The hay, or long grass, fell into even swathes, a fact that was noted by John in his critical and continuing commentary on his work.

John was an expert at repairing old rail fences. His skills generally ran to repairs, rather than to original construction, and to building sheds rather than building houses and substantial barns. When a neighbor of mine for whom John had rebuilt on old rail fence raised questions about the stability of the finished work, John assured him that "that fence ain't going any place." The old fence is gone now and a new one has been erected in its place. Consistent with his role, John had prolonged the life of the fence until its total demise.

He did the same for houses. Usually he was the last tenant before abandonment.

This gift of prolonging useful life, until final disposal, was demonstrated in other ways than of saving fences and houses for a few years. John could get a year of two of service out of a pickup truck after all others had despaired of any such success. One of his final acts, before his death, was to buy a new pickup truck, pledging his old truck and his other assets and income to pay for the new truck. Foreclosure followed in three months, and John returned for transportation to a salvaged truck again.

John was a grave digger for those who favored traditional, hand dug graves to the modern type, excavated by a backhoe. Beyond the grave John dealt with animals and the supernatural, or at least preternatural. His reports of having seen mountain lions were believed. Reports by others were generally questioned. His ghost stories were treated as credible. At least three of them were. One was an experience he had had when he entered an abandoned house to avoid a rain storm while hunting. John did not report having seen the ghost, but that he had been touched by it, and had fled into the rainy night.

The second was an experience had while riding with his father in a wagon being pulled by a team of mules. According to John, as they passed a graveyard adjacent to a country church, something came out of the yard and jumped onto to the back of the mules. The mules bolted and raced up the road until they reached the church, when the thing or things jumped off the backs of the mules. John heard the thump as the ghosts landed on the road. The mules immediately slowed to a walk.

John's third ghost story involved a haunted car. The car, before John bought it, had been involved in a strange death, murder or suicide. The car had operated normally as John drove it home after the purchase. After dark strange things began to happen. The headlights came on and the brake lights. The windshield wiper became active. The horn sounded. The starter growled but the car did not start. John fled to the shelter of the house. The next morning he maneuvered the car to the edge of a ravine, removed the tires, which evidently he thought were not haunted, and pushed the car into the ravine.

John was much like Paddy Flynn, a character described by W.B. Yeats , in his book The Celtic Twilight, as a teller of tales, always cheerful, but marked by underlying melancholy, a visionary melancholy which is a part of the joy, Yeats says, of purely instinctive natures.

The Most Trusted People

… in the Judgment of the Residents of Rappahannock County

MOVED BY *TIME* MAGAZINE'S announcement that for 1982 it would pick no person of the year, but rather the "computer," as a more significant force in that year than any person, and noting that George Gallup, *Good Housekeeping Magazine,* and other institutions were publishing their selections of the most "admired," most "trusted," and other superlative qualities, I decided that it would be worthwhile to make a study to determine who in the estimation of residents of Rappahannock County were most trusted as 1982 ended.

Rappahannock County provides a good base area for such an inquiry. It is 75 miles from Washington, the capital of the United States, just beyond commuter range, and only marginally within range of Washington's television stations. Subscribers to *The Washington Post* are few and subscribers to *The New York Times,* even fewer.

Its western border is the Blue Ridge Mountains. Its eastern border is the Rappahannock River, first made famous in the story that George Washington once threw a stone across it. It is a county noted for its independence, first shown at the time of the War Between The States, when the loyalty to the South of many of its citizens was at best marginal. It has maintained its reputation for independence despite a modest influx of retired military personnel, newspaper persons, both retired and active, airline pilots and flight attendants, and others. Some proper Virginians refer to Rappahannock County as the Free State of Rappahannock.

The committee designated to supervise the inquiry resolved that its study would be scientific, more thorough, more free of possible prejudice than other similar studies, and that its findings would be socially more significant than those of other reports.

"Trust" was to be the key word. "Trust," the committee decided, was a much more important attribute or quality than say "admiration." The committee also decided that "trust" as a generalization was too vague, and that its inquiry should be restricted to important areas and relationships which call for different kinds of trust, or trust in greater measure than is required in other cases.

Politics was excluded as a general category in which trustworthiness might be evaluated, as too broad; but politicians were allowed in the competition in other categories. Doctors and lawyers were also excluded, first because early inquiries established that persons generally trust whatever doctor or lawyer they are involved with. Beyond that the basis for trust in doctors and lawyers is their professional identification. Theoretically every doctor, allowing for specialization, and every lawyer, again allowing for specialization, should be as qualified as every other one in that specialty, just as dog experts in Rappahannock County say every Beagle is expected to behave like every other Beagle.

Having made these exceptions the committee selected ten categories of human relationships of some dependency, in which trust is important.
1. Judgment in court.
2. Religious counsel and inspiration.
3. Communication of news, either to one, or about one.

4. Personal security, or help, in time of danger, the ultimate element of national security and defense.
5. Protection within the environment, and its preservation, including the world itself.
6. Some certainty about what one consumes, eats, or uses.
7. An assured, safe, and adequate supply of water, and other liquids.
8. Confidence in others for care of children, of the sick, of the aged, or of cherished possessions, including one's house and pets.
9. The important matter of automobile purchase, new or used, operation, and repair.
10. Certainty of privacy, of reliability, in the care of one's messages, gifts, and the like, when in transit, or otherwise out of one's personal sight or control.

The methods used in determining the attitudes and judgments of the people of Rappahannock County were indirect and subtle. There was no direct mail. There were no intrusive telephone calls, no house visits, no confrontations on the street. The opinions were gathered quietly, unobtrusively, in country stores, before and after church services, in post offices, during fox hunts, in the woods while cutting wood, in filling stations, at the Volunteer Firemen's bingo games, and in like situations.

In each of the fields of trust to be tested one Rappahannock resident was entered, against the field, the world. These were the results.

In the first test category, the judicial one, the basic question asked was "Whom would you like to have as judge if you were brought into court?" The easy winner was retired Judge Rayner Snead, who ran well ahead of all other judges entered, including Chief Justice Warren Burger, Associate Justice Sandra O'Connor, or Judge John Sirica of Watergate fame.

The poll showed that generally Judge Snead was first choice because of his record in settling inter-family feuds, approaching in intensity that of the Hatfields and McCoys in some cases, and beyond that of settling intra-family feuds, which can be even more serious. It was also noted that he is masterful in settling boundary disputes, evidently knowing that fences move in this county in strange ways, and also taking into account the fact that much of the county was surveyed by George Washington who, it appears, was less than a perfect surveyor. There are some in the county who hold that if George had surveyed the Mason Dixon line, the War Between The States might never have occurred for lack of certainty as to which side of the line one lived on.

The final testimony as to the trustworthiness of Judge Snead came from those who play tennis with him. They said that he was fully reliable in making tennis calls, even when the game was played on his own court; going beyond, these observers said, the accepted Rappahannock rules that allow the owner of the court to call the game, and also allow him, or her, to shade the calls slightly in his or her own favor.

In the religious trust competition the winner was the Reverend Jennings Hobson, of the Episcopal Church of Washington, the county seat. Hobson ran well ahead of Pope John Paul II who led the list of most admired men in the Gallup survey of 1980 and was second in that study in 1981. The number of Catholics, it was noted by outside consultants, is small in Rappahannock County. Rev. Hobson also ran well ahead of Billy Graham who was fourth in the Gallup findings in both 1980 and 1981. Hobson also outscored Oral Roberts, who a few irreligious persons in the county thought was a basketball coach, and also bested Jerry Falwell of Lynchburg, Virginia. The significant test point that distinguished Rev. Hobson was, for some, the fact that he regularly blesses the hounds at the opening of the hunt season.

In the third range of contest, communications, it was Daphne Hutchinson, of the *Rappahannock News,* against the likes of Dan Rather, Barbara Walters, and James Reston of *The New York Times,* and also Walter Cronkite, now retired, but who was included because a few years ago he was considered in one poll as the most trusted man in America. Daphne was judged to be the complete communicator, one who does her own reporting, her own editing, and who also takes and selects the pictures which accompany her writings. In response to the question "Of all of these persons, which would you want to write your obituary?" the choice of Daphne was unanimous.

The controlling question in making choices in the fourth category of personal and national security was "Whom would you like to have come into view, say, following a nuclear attack: The Commander in Chief of the Armed Services, Ronald Reagan, in a helicopter; or Caspar Weinberger, the Secretary of Defense, in an M1 tank; or Carrol Jenkins of Sperryville in his pickup truck?" The choice was again unanimous for Carrol.

The fifth area in which the search for the most trusted person in the county was conducted was marked by complexity and difficulty. Protection of the environment extends from very limited concerns over such things as endangered insects, somewhat in the manner of Albert Schweitzer, to preserving the earth itself as a habitable planet, the concern of Robert Heilbroner, who in his book published a few years ago projected that human life on the earth might cease within one hundred and fifty years, because of population pressure, and/or nuclear war, the warming or cooling of the atmosphere (I forget which) and other threatening developments. Heilbroner has since given the earth an extension of time.

One of the entries in this competition was Lady Bird Johnson, who as First Lady and since has shown an interest in environment, and in beautification, and who was once cited in a poem concerned about ecology, especially the relationship of bees to fruits, flowers, and berries. The poem was inspired by the need to defend a quota on foreign honey against ridicule of television correspondents, so that the United States' bee keepers would not be discouraged and stop keeping bees. This is a relationship understood in Rappahannock County, where orchards of apples and peaches thrive.

This is the poem:
Now a quota on honey
May seem very funny
To people who talk on T V.
But consider the tree
In need of a bee

To insure its posterity
The standard Manhattan
Without a cherry
And no lemon peel
For the dry Martini
The empty hive, the exiled queen
The disconsolate drone
The last clover sown
And in search of one flower
Lady Bird wandering
Through that dismal gray
Desolate, terminal Spring.

James Watt was an entry, out of token recognition of his office at that time of Secretary of the Interior, and also Anne Gorsuch Burford, the then head of the Environmental Protection Agency. Neither scored well.

Former President Carter was included, primarily on the basis of a strong pro-environment statement he made while President, when he said, "We must stop the despoiling or derogating of the land or of the air or the water within which we live."

The person to be trusted with the environment above all others, those polled in Rappahannock County concluded, was Lyt Woods, former county forester. Weighing heavily in Lyt's favor was his understanding of prime lumbers, and their relationship to the cycle of both the 17-year locust and the 13-year locust, his knowledge of the problems of the chestnut oak, and his mastery of the hammer dulcimer, a becoming instrument for an environment protector.

For want of pure and plentiful water, wars have been fought, fertile lands have become deserts, nations have disappeared. Even the survival of Washington, Virginia, population about 200, the county seat of Rappahannock County, was threatened two years ago for want of water.

In pagan cultures the water spirits were revered and worshiped. In all civilizations the person who could find and produce water has been honored. The Rappahannock County entry in this competition which was not only worldwide, but history long, was a marginal outsider, Larry LeHew, the well digger from adjoining Warren County, Virginia. Larry was qualified because he has been accepted as the joint master of the Rappahannock Hunt, a singular honor, and because he knows the terrain of the county, has dug many wells in the county, but especially for his achievement in finding a full-flowing well, thus saving "Little Washington" when all others had despaired.

Larry is a thorough water seeker. He is willing to use the help of dowsers, of prayer, of geologists from the University of Virginia, and then go it on his own. Since there was no contemporary world quality opposition to Larry, a few write-ins for Moses were accepted. Larry contends that there is reason to believe that Moses struck a good many rocks with his rod, without success, before he finally hit the right one in the desert and saved the Israelites.

A further test and demonstration of Larry LeHew's trustworthiness occurred just after the water began to flow from the new well in Washington. When word came that the water could not be put on line in the city water system until approved by the Virginia Department of Health, Larry lay down in the mud, drank the rising water and declared that it was perfect, fit for human use - all facts later sustained by the state testers. Larry is also qualified to give advice and counsel on other potables.

Choosing a most trusted consumer protector was a serious challenge because of the number of specialists in the field and because of the wide range of human needs that seem to have attracted protectors. In order to get meaningful results, the supervisors of this poll decided to set the county contestant against individual, specialized protectors, and also against a composite of all entries.

Harvey Gordon, supported by his wife Jean, of H and J Grocery, represented the county against this dual opposition and was judged to be more trustworthy than any one of his opponents or the composite.

Harvey does not over-protect. But he is reliable and predictable. If Harvey has once had some piece of merchandise, he almost certainly will have it the next time someone asks for it. He may drop an item occasionally, but not without giving warning that he intends to do so, or telling prospective buyers that he has done so, and further that he does not intend to replace it. If a customer asks for something Harvey does not have he is likely to be advised that Harvey does not have it, never has had it, and never intends to have it. If one asks Harvey to reserve a Sunday paper, he will, and keep it for months waiting for the call.

Harvey demonstrated his concern for consumers in his optimism about gasoline prices, by being the last, or one of the last, in the county to change the mechanism on his pumps so that they recorded prices in excess of one dollar a gallon. Harvey stuck with the old indicators, notifying customers that the cost of a gallon of gasoline was twice that registered on the pumps, but that he looked forward to the day when multiplication would not be necessary.

Harvey's service to consumers or potential consumers goes beyond food, drink, tools, and other items of trade. He also advises on weather, on road conditions, on hunting prospects (during the season), and on how the horses are running at Charles Town, West Virginia.

Entered against Harvey, singly and in concert, were Nancy Steorts, Chairman of the Reagan Consumer Product Safety Commission; John Gardner of Common Cause, who has undertaken the difficult task of protecting all of us from ourselves and from democracy; Father Drinan, head of the Americans for Democratic Action, an organization originally established in the late 1940s to protect liberals from communists, which now has a separate committee that studies and reports to the country on dangerous toys, unfair toy prices, and on toys that might have an adverse psychological effect on children and, one can assume, on adults who play with the same toys.

The Avon Lady was a participant in the test, along with Ronald McDonald, Frank Perdue, and Ralph Nader.

In the eighth category of trust the choice was clear, easy, and early. Affie Andes and her husband were chosen as the persons to whom you would trust the care, cleaning, and preservation of cherished household goods, or a house, or its dependent inhabitants: children, the sick, the aged, and animals. The Andes's deserved choice is based on the fact that when they care for things or persons, they do so gently. They clean in the English fashion, expecting things to last for generations. They replace things just as they were, with no re-arranging of cupboards. They object to using liquid wax on floors, and refuse to wash windows on one side only. Their institutional opposition was "Mr. Clean" of advertising fame. Their personal challengers, at high levels, were the former mistress of the White House, Rosalynn Carter, and her successor as manager, or caretaker, Nancy Reagan.

Possibly the closest competition for the Rappahannock person to be trusted to represent the county in the world contest was the person to whom one would go for advice in purchasing a new or a used car, or for repair or servicing. Garagemen and automobile mechanics in Rappahannock, we found, have strong supporters. It was the conclusion of the group supervising this poll that any number of persons might have been entered from the county and won against the world. A choice had to be made. It fell to the Baldwin Brothers of Sperryville to carry the county banner. They carried it well in a multiple test against strong competition. In the new car selection they successfully defeated John De Lorean, of North Ireland, and Lee Iacocca, of Chrysler and television fame. In the selection of a used car, they were chosen over former President Nixon, with the carrying question: "Which of these persons would you buy a used car from?"

In the special contest over repairs and service, the Baldwin Brothers took on the tag team of Mr. Midas and Mr. Goodwrench. They won. The fact that the Baldwins or some of their relatives also deal in hides, furs, and ginseng did not seem to be a measurable factor, either positive or negative, in the support they received relative to the automobile. John Glasker of Hawlin Hollow was considered in a separate test as the best man to go to if you had a car which you believed would never run again.

The final test was that of a most subtle trust, basically of one's privacy, secret thoughts, words, communications, goods, of involvements of highly personal and sensitive nature, which at some point have to be entrusted to some other person.

Bankers were considered, beginning with David Rockefeller of Chase Manhattan Bank. Judge Webster, head of the Federal Bureau of Investigation, was included, along with the commissioner of Internal Revenue, and income tax advisor H. R. Block. Margaret Thatcher, Prime Minister of England, was also included because she is responsible for the British Royal Mail and for British Intelligence secrecy. Western Union and the Bell Telephone Company were entered in the non-person class, along with Time magazine's 1982 winner of the year, the computer. William Bolger, the Postmaster General of the United States, finished last.

Whereas the judges concluded that the postal service of the country was not fully reliable, they allowed that one unit of it was, the Woodville Post Office run by Mrs. Lacey Orange. She and her carriers were held to be most trustworthy as protectors of private things delivered to her - letters, as well as goods, not just ordinary perishable things such as ham or cheese, but things that can perish absolutely such as baby chickens and bees sent through the mail. In its commitment to deliver, the Woodville Post Office and its personnel go far beyond the slogan of the U.S. Post Office. To that slogan - "Neither Snow, Nor Rain, Nor Heat, Nor Gloom of Night Stops These Couriers From the Swift Completion of Their Appointed Rounds" - Mrs. Orange and her carriers make it possible to add "Nor Rappahannock mud, nor ice on Routes 621 and 618."

County Justice

The Jail at Washington, Virginia

JURIES are not quick to find persons guilty in this part of Virginia, nor are judges generally noted as harsh or hanging judges. Justice is tempered by experience, common sense, a sensitivity to extenuating circumstances such as passion or property rights, the latter being much respected. The judgment of one's peers is generally trusted. Two recent cases in the area did not run quite true to form. One involved a coon hound case, which went as far as the circuit court; the other, a man found guilty of illegally selling alcoholic beverages.

In the first case, one Fred Payne brought suit, claiming that he had lost a valuable Blue Tick coon hound called variously "Blue Ann"; "Bugle Ann"; or sometimes just plain "Ann" without an "e"; and sometimes, even more plainly and generically, "Coon Hound." Evidently she is never called just "Hound," "Dog," or even "Hound Dog."

Payne charged that one William Ernest Brown would not allow Payne to go searching for his dog in a field that Brown was renting.

The case was especially complicated because on this night in early March, Payne had let Bugle Ann and two other dogs out on the trail. The other two dogs were fox hounds. The reason for running Bugle Ann with the fox hounds is one well recognized by coon hunters. Payne, according to his testimony, wanted to see if his coon dog was in good form and would not be distracted and go off to chase a fox. If she did, she would be disqualified in the coon hound competition he intended to enter her in very soon, down in Orangeburg, South Carolina. Other coon hound handlers testified that Payne was following accepted practice, especially if he was going to go four or five hundred miles for a competitive hunt.

Payne did have permission to hunt on the land adjoining the property Brown was renting. Evidently, or possibly not evidently, Bugle Ann followed a fox onto Brown's land. But before Payne could find her in the forbidden fields, Brown, supported by a deputy sheriff, intervened. Payne was informed that under Virginia law, which he already knew, the owner had the right to go on any land to retrieve a dog, if the owner was not carrying a gun. Payne was not. Yet he was dissuaded from doing so by the deputy's statement that if he did go onto the Brown land, he would be arrested for trespassing.

According to Payne, he waited by the fence for about a half-hour hoping that Ann would return to him. She did not. Payne asked $5,000.00 in damages, a claim supported by Russell Hamm of the Blue Tick Association of America who testified that Hamm had sold Bugle Ann to Payne a year earlier for $4,000.00 and the trade of a dog Payne owned. Said Hamm, "I allowed him $1,000.00 and sold the dog for $1,250.00."

The judge instructed the jury that if they were to find for Payne and Bugle Ann, the jury should be assured that Payne would have found his dog if he had been allowed on the Brown land. The jury held against Payne.

The general judgment of coon dog handlers and of coon hunters was that this was a serious miscarriage of justice and that the judge, who claimed some knowledge of bird dogs, was unqualified to pass judgment himself or to instruct a jury in a case involving a coon hound. In Rappahannock County, bird dogs have little standing and are seldom mentioned in either the same breath or same sentence or even same conversation with coon dogs.

The second case also did involve a miscarriage of justice, according to local opinion; but that miscarriage was pretty well balanced by the sentence which was imposed and by the manner, intensity, and thoroughness with which it has been enforced.

In Virginia, bottle liquor is sold legally only through state liquor stores. Rappahannock County has no such store. Consequently anyone in need of a bottle of liquor must travel twenty to thirty miles, if he starts from the center of the county, to satisfy his needs or wants. He may take the trip over the mountains to Luray in Page County, going west. He may go north to Front Royal in Warren County. He may go south to Madison in Madison County or southeast to Culpeper in Culpeper County. This point was made with clarity and emphasis by lawyer Jim Bill Fletcher in defense of his client, Usters Benton Dodson. Usters is what is called an F.T. Valley man. ("F.T. Valley" is a valley named after Francis Thornton, one of the early settlers in the area. Thornton also has a gap named after him, a river, a church, and a number of descendants.) This was Usters' fourth appearance before a court on the same offense, namely that he was selling liquor without a proper Virginia Alcoholic Beverage Control license. Usters was found out, exposed, and charged by State Police Inspector Schultze. The judge sentenced Usters - not the Police Inspector, as some thought he should have done - to sixty days in jail, a sentence to be suspended in exchange for 240 hours of community service.

A related charge of possessing firearms while selling illegal alcohol was dropped when the firearms in question were found to be part of Usters' gun collection.

There is no clear ruling as to how many guns one must have in the county before the guns in question stop being firearms and become part of a gun collection.

It was acknowledged by the court that the liquor Usters was selling was legal liquor, but it was being sold illegally. The Virginia alcohol tax had been paid. It was not moonshine. The total stock consisted of two fifths of opened Canadian Mist, which the judge ordered destroyed; 39 gallons of whiskey, presumably Bourbon; 4 gallons of wine; and 38 gallons of beer, all of which the judge ordered be returned or handed over to the State of Virginia.

Rappahannock County is not much into moonshine production, although those on the inside generally can find local peach or apple brandy. Franklin County in southwestern Virginia is better known as a production area for moonshine, where the illegal liquor production operates on delicate economic lines, reflecting changes in the price of domestic corn, in the price of sugar in the world market, and even slight changes in the liquor taxes of Virginia and of neighboring states.

At last report, Usters was still at large, because the county attorney said there were no community sites established in Rappahannock County where he might serve society.

The whittlers at the Corner Store in Sperryville agreed that what Usters had been arrested for was probably the best community service he could perform, especially in a time of high gasoline prices and when there was growing concern over the problem of drivers who might be drinking on the road after having driven thirty or forty miles to get a bottle.

Washington, VA. Courthouse Grounds
& Confederate Monument

Picking Presidential Candidates Rappahannock Style

IT IS GETTING MORE AND MORE DIFFICULT to distinguish among presidential candidates, not only within one or the other of the two major parties, but also between candidates of the two parties. The issues are confusing. Party and candidate positions change almost daily.

In order to keep campaigns in some focus and to evaluate and sort out candidates along the way, with the help of county experts, I have compiled a set of ten standards, possibly commandments, all of which are separate from the candidates' stands on issues but bear significantly on his or her capacity to be the President of the United States.

Any candidate is likely to fail on one or two of these ten standards, but a candidate found wanting on as many as five should be considered as having questionable qualifications for the Presidency.

The ten Rappahannock standards are these:

1. Did the Candidate announce in February?

Such an announcement shows serious lack of good judgment. February has long been recognized as a month in which no serious decisions or announcements should be made. The early Romans dedicated February to the lower world. In that month they worshipped Pluto and the souls of their dead ancestors. They looked down and backward rather than forward. It was for them a time of no decision. Medieval Christians had a similar attitude towards February; they viewed it as the worst of months. Even a "fair" February was frowned upon as noted in a Welsh proverb saying "A Welshman would rather see his mother dead, than see a fair February."

Animals also shun decision-making in February. It is a month of deep hibernation. Only the groundhog, by reputation, breaks out on one day to make a simple decision and then returns to hibernation.

2. Does he make his announcement surrounded or backed up by his wife, or husband, and/or children?

The Presidency, we have been told, is a lonely office. The announcement of candidacy for the office should be the same. If any candidate includes the family dog, or dogs, he or she should be doubly discounted. Dogs are well thought of in Rappahannock County, and not to be used carelessly or for political purposes. A dog may be used as a witness for the defense of a politician who is in trouble. And, of course, if a candidate's dog is attacked the candidate not only has the right to defend the dog, but the duty to do so.

3. Does the candidate, as the sole auditor, frequently quote politicians who have passed away, or represent himself as continuing the tradition of such politicians, in a way standing in for them, in a kind of reincarnation?

4. Does the candidate frequently quote the Bible, not casually, but giving chapter and verse?

5. Does the candidate claim that he or she has received a sudden inspiration, either religious or reasoned, to run for the Presidency?

6. Does the candidate publish income tax returns, financial records, or medical reports, and challenge others to do the same - a case of self-serving, indecent over-exposure?

7. Does the candidate promise that he or she will pick a blue ribbon cabinet, rather than say, a red ribbon one, or green ribbon cabinet?

8. Is the candidate a former Vice-President of whom it was said "he has given the office new meaning," rather than one who looked upon the office as did Thomas Jefferson, as giving him time in the winter to meditate on philosophy and in the summer to study nature and who did not waste his years as Vice-President trying to give the office new meaning, but spent it constructively, inventing among other things a leather buggy top and a better plough?

Numbers nine and ten are more subtle, and somewhat difficult to apply, in the same way that the last two of the Decalogue - the ninth and tenth - are difficult to apply and to obey.

9. The ninth raises questions about any candidate who has engaged in sports or other activities that cause his oxygen supply to vary significantly above or below normal, as in scuba diving, or mountain climbing, or marathon running, intense jogging, possibly submarine service or work in outer space, where oxygen must be supplied artificially.

10. The last test is especially difficult to apply. It raises the question of whether the candidate knows that pigs and cattle have to be handled differently. If one is attempting to drive cows, he or she must start them slowly, sing to them, and gradually speed up the drive to near stampede level, as one gets them where he wants them. (The House of Representatives is best handled by this method.) Pigs on the other hand must be startled into action under panic conditions, through shouting at them, preferably in Latin, beating on the pig troughs or on the fence, and then gradually slowing down the pace of the drive until the pigs arrive at the appointed place, at a slow walk, believing that they had made choices along the way. The hog driving technique is preferred in moving the Senate to action. The candidate should also know that in cold weather a pig will do almost anything to keep its nose warm. The remains of five pigs were once discovered in a glacier, frozen to death in a circle.

An Endangered Species: The Rural Mail Box

FIVE YEARS AGO I noted what I thought was a threat to the Rural Mail Box. I feared that it had become an endangered species, not as birds or beasts, or fish or flowers, or weeds, or trees, are threatened by blight or mold, or spreading suburbs and freeways, or industrial growth or new dams or waterways, as in the case of the louse wont and the snail darter, but by the Insurance Institute of Highway Safety.

The Insurance Institute had discovered that under some conditions the roadside Rural Free Delivery mail boxes, together with their sustaining posts, supports, and mountings, were a threat to the life and limb of some automobile drivers and passengers, and might do damage to the automobile itself, to say nothing of the insurance companies.

On the basis of limited study and what it called "sketchy data," the Institute published a "Status Report" charging that mail boxes were a serious roadside hazard. The report was taken up by the United States Postal Service, which, stirred by the results of the Texas study and by the report of the Insurance Institute, announced that it was "looking into the whole matter" in order "to explore the possibility of establishing safety requirements for mail box supports," an example of how some of the things done by government are begun by non-governmental institutions, by private businesses, and especially by the institutes supported by private businesses.

The Insurance Institute announced that it would continue to sponsor research in the hope of developing safe mail boxes and safe mountings.

I anticipated that a soft plastic mail box like those given to country newspaper subscribers by publishers, a new design, certainly, without the classical lines of the standard U.S. mail box available at hardware stores and from mail order houses, in basic unpainted galvanized gray, or painted black would be required. I expected that standard specifications as to placement, height of standards, composition and shape of supporting structures, a new color, scientifically tested so as not to attract the attention of any automobile drivers, might be forthcoming.

I expected that cedar posts commonly used as supports for mail boxes in wetlands would have to go, as well as solid oak in temperate zones on reasonably high ground. The trusted locust, the only sure post in termite and dry rot zones, would be banned and cantilevered mountings declared illegal.

At the time, the Postal Service spokesman said, "I don't think anyone knows how large the problem might be."

I feared the worst, but now five years after the early studies there is no evidence that the Postal Department has made any moves. The problem may have been greater than those who instituted and pursued the study anticipated. Counter studies may have shown how many lives were saved because rural mail boxes of various shapes and colors, on a variety of mountings along the road, have kept sleepy drivers awake, have warned persons driving in a fog of either mist or alcohol of where the road ended and where the ditch began, or have marked in snow blown plains the line between road and field, and of how drivers alerted and forewarned by hitting mail boxes have been saved from the worse fate of running into ditches, or hitting trees, or rocky banks.

In any case I note that the standard box still survives, and that personal tastes, and creativity, are still allowed in choice of boxes and in placement and in mountings. In this county "Uncle Sams," cut out of board or plank, offer boxes to the mail man or woman. Old walking ploughs, set in cement with boxes mounted at the beam's end, are in evidence, as are boxes held between wheels, salvaged from hay rakes and cultivators. The welded chain support, sure to draw attention, has some adherents. Boxes mounted on pipes set in milk cans filled with cement, which can be set up again when knocked down by cars or snow ploughs, survive, as do boxes painted in any but the "official colors," and miniatures of house, or barn, and even of country churches. The locust post remains the dominant support, at least in Rappahannock County.

CULTURE & COMFORT

The F.T. Valley Grocery Store

The F.T. Valley Grocery Store is the first grocery store on Route 231 as the road turns west from Sperryville towards Madison, Virginia. It is located just at the point that the valley opens to the west and is named, or initialed after a pioneer settler, Frances Thornton. A gap in the Blue Mountain range and the river that runs down from the gap also bear his name.

The store is operated by Wilma Burke. Most stores in western Rappahannock County are operated by members of the Burke family or by their relatives. This store was identified until a few years ago by the initials of the first names of the operators, W & J, and before that H & J. Wilma changed to F.T. as a more permanent name, one that had served the valley for two or more centuries.

The store is more than a grocery. It includes a sandwich and lunch service, a coffee bar, a modest wine list and an extensive supply of beer, three of four kinds of bottled water and an ice dispenser, a modest drug store, and a modest hardware supply of essentials like mouse traps and brooms. There is a clothing department featuring T-shirts and special caps and three gasoline pumps, and a supply of "if you don's see it, ask for it" items. It also features a newspaper rack which supplies local and Virginia major papers, and *The Washington Post* and *The New York Times*.

In the midst of all this commerce there is a morning discussion group fuelled by morning coffee, which includes over the course of six days (Wilma recently initiated a "closed on Sunday" policy which was like having the church close) a horseman or two, a game warden, the county animal control officer, an occasional highway patroller or deputy sheriff, retired military officers, mostly colonels, some historians (academic and lay), including one from each of the last three major wars, cattle dealers and farmers, school bus drivers, a lawyer, a doctor, a woodcutter or two, an apple grower, the principal used-car dealer of the county, two retired firemen and civil service employees, and one or two persons whose professions and work are unknown or at least not publicly acknowledged. Moonshining is not unknown to the county, and poaching, especially involving aphrodisiacs like bear parts, rattle snake meat, and, for vegetarians, ginseng. Russ Limbaugh is quoted more often than is the *New York Times*.

The issue of school discipline was hotly debated for several days, Charlie, the schoolbus driver maintaining that school discipline begins on the bus, the morning bus, and ends on the evening one. This debate was extended to include the matter of prayer in public lower schools and before football games at state supported institutions of higher learning. One historian stated in support of his pro-prayer position that Notre Dame in the 2000 season had beaten every state institution it had played after the Supreme Court had forbidden those schools to pray before games.

The solution of the problem, at the lower school level, was to have prayers but to have them said on the busses since the persons favoring busing are, as a rule, opposed to prayer in public schools. Those opposed to busing, as a rule, favor prayer. Charlie thought that this compromise might work .

A second topic of serious concern to the group, one that most members felt not given the attention it deserved, was gun control. The division was sharp, the National Rifle faction being willing to accept gun sizes beginning at the canon level: the gun control faction unwilling to allow any weapons beyond those in existence when the second amendment was adopted; namely, muzzle loader rifles and flintlock pistols, which they thought Justice Scali would approve as meeting the test of original intent. Between these extremes there was a variety of positions and proposals, some based on number of bullets in the magazine, the caliber of bullets, length of the gunbarrels, etc.

There was no settlement of the issue, but the controversy spilled over into that of what to do about the irresponsibility and unfairness of the press. This was not an intrusion since the Press questions its own performance, much in the way monkeys in the zoo get into bouts of self examination and of mutual examination, scratching themselves and each other, tasting what they find, eating it, or offering it to other monkeys. The desperate conclusion was that the only effective reform would be the restoration of the duel, the recourse one James Shields (Illinois politician and later a Senator from Minnesota) had in dealing with a remark Abraham Lincoln made, equating Shields' oratory with the wisps of cat hair floating about after a cat fight. Weapons and place were chosen but the duel called off by intervening, cooler heads.

The question of what to do about automobile theft was considered at the request of the used car dealer , Buster Hitt. The conclusion was that anyone who steals a car should be charged the Hertz rates given a second-hand car, preferably Buster's stock, and required to support it for life. The cost of chasing stolen cars, arresting car thieves, holding them in jails, convicting them and keeping them in prison would be greatly reduced, it was argued.

Since Rappahannock County was Mosley territory during the Civil War, support for restoration of the cavalry as a major military reform received strong support from the group The reasons for support were varied. Some held that a restored cavalry would attract frustrated and potential polo players who might otherwise go into the CIA where they might only cause trouble. Some believed that the conditioning, feeding, grooming and training of the equine units would distract military personnel from contingency war planning and that it would encourage high level disarmament. And that the losses to the defense economy caused by the elimination or reduction of high-tech procurement would be offset by growth in saddle-making, blacksmithing and by the increased production of oats and hay. Women were not formally excluded from the meeting but did not find the accommodations very inviting.

Their participation was largely limited to reporting lost and strayed dogs to the dog warden and attacks by marauding bears on bird-feeders, bluebird houses and peach trees to the game warden. The seven plagues that visit the county are discussed at the meetings, but, since there is no official in the group who is responsible for insects, deer ticks, wood ticks, gypsy moths pine-bark beetles, seven and thirteen year locusts, tent caterpillars, and lady bugs receive only passing attention.

Politics has received less and less attention since the inauguration of President Bush (43). The strongest Democrat refers to him as "the Pretender". Buster Hitt, the used-car salesman, who is given to using metaphors drawn from the automobile world, has observed that the President's clutch seems to be slipping, and Wilma has rejected an offer to have her give the *Washington Post* and the *New York Times* free to her customers every time the respective papers carry a picture of the President on the front page, and that she in turn be paid double whenever the front page does not have a Presidential picture. The last straw forcing her decision was the picture of the President carrying his dog, Barney, off the airplane.

Consumers Dis-Union

Divided We Stand

CONSUMER PROTECTION is not given a very high priority among the matters of concern to the residents of Rappahannock County. Major purchases such as used cars, land, houses, horses, and cattle are usually based on the buyer's knowledge of what he or she is buying or on trust in the seller, with little or no help from organizations like Consumers Union. Consequently the recent publication of that organization's 50-year retrospective, entitled I'll Buy That, did not stir much response in the county-especially since the 50 "small wonders and big deals" which the editors of the publication said had revolutionized the lives of consumers had at best a marginal effect on the lives of consumers in Rappahannock County.

Of the 50 items emphasized in the book, ten involve automobiles, including the introduction of the seat belt. There is no evidence as to what effect the belt has had on life in the county, but of the other nine, including such innovations as the automatic transmission, only one, the jeep, or four-wheel drive vehicle, has had any noticeable effect on the way of life in the county.

The effects of enriched bread, tampons, Dr. Spock's baby book, disposable diapers, the pill, and fluoridized water, all considered by Consumers Union to have significant national impact, have not had measurable impact in the county. Nor have various sound and picture recording, reproducing, and transmitting devices, such as T.V., compact discs, hi fi's, LP records, transistors, magnetic tapes, VCRs or satellite dishes, although most are in evidence and in use in the county.

Detergents have replaced homemade soap, a scarcely revolutionary change. Air travel in and out of the county is limited to what may be handled by one grass landing strip. Suburbia has not yet reached the county. There is no McDonald's, no supermarket, and no real shopping mall. Credit cards, excepting for purchase of gasoline, are not widely in use. Checks for all purposes are commonly made out to "cash."

Power lawn mowers, according to Consumers Union, have had a significant effect on suburban development and suburban living. This phenomenon has encouraged larger lawns, thus providing exercise for suburbanites, practically destroying Sunday as a day of rest, and leading to the formulation of great principles of community living such as "Never trust a neighbor who offers to cut your lawn or trim your side of a hedge." Lawns may be slightly larger and better kept with the grass cut shorter than it was when cut by hay mowers or bush hogs, but power mowers have had at most a marginal effect in the county.

More significant than the new products and institutions which have had little or no effect in the county are those which have been resisted, for good reasons and with social and community benefits. Among these are three of special note: air-conditioning, the electric dryer, and running shoes.

Air conditioning, according to product analysts, and societal psychologists, has eliminated the differences between the sun belt and the snow belt. Also eliminated, or in the process of being eliminated, are both open and screened porches, front and back, thus doing away with a traditional courting place with minimal family supervision and leaving only the automobile as the place for this important social rite.

Rappahannock County is not in the snow belt or in the sun belt. It is in what might best be called the "sleet belt." Air-conditioning has not caught on here. Nor has the porch, which has been a part of houses in this area, been eliminated. Both screened porches and open porches are common on old houses and on newly built ones, both front and back, and sometimes on three sides with a deck added on the fourth for good measure. More substantial older houses not only had porches at ground level, but also on the second story.

Mainstreet Porch

Porches in Rappahannock are not limited in use to one or two functions. They serve multiple purposes, the standard one of shade and protection from rain; the social one of sitting and talking and watching; an additional one of providing storage space for washing machines and other household equipment and utensils; for wood storage during the winter; for display of flowers, especially hanging pots of geraniums; also for pottery, ceramic and pressed concrete animals and birds; with open space beneath the porch floor used for more storage, plus home or haven for dogs and cats.

The electric washer and dryer, in the opinion of Consumers Union, have had significant national effect. The washer has been accepted and is widely used in the county, but it functions in a way little different from the earlier hand-washing machines. The dryer has had no such acceptance. Clothes of many shapes, colors, and uses still hang on backyard clothes lines on Monday and Tuesday, the traditional days for drying clothes. Drying is done by sun and wind, and the social good of talk across backyard fences is preserved.

Running shoes (once called tennis shoes) have made a revolutionary mark in backward countries where they have become standard footwear, and also among women in more advanced societies. Once the shoes of "little old ladies in tennis shoes," they have been taken over by emancipated professional and paraprofessional women (at least on the way to work and on the way home) as a mark of independence from the hobbling custom imposed by high-heeled shoes. The use of running shoes has brought on the manufacture and marketing of at least one new product, now advertised on television, designed to neutralize the odor of walking or running shoes at home, in carrying bags, or in office file cabinets. "Odor Eater," one such product, is a far cry from the reality of twenty-five years ago when in late summer, a boy's "Keds" became so rank that mothers ordered them put out of doors at night along with the cat. Running shoes have made some inroads in Rappahannock County especially in their use by women, but the basic and dominating footwear is still the calf-length, unlined, snake proof, leather Rappahannock County boot.

Consumers Union should not be too disappointed in the failure of Rappahannock County residents to conform to the Union's findings, keeping in mind that the produce buyer in Sperryville buys Genseng, and live rattlesnakes.

Where Old Cars Go

Rappahannock Retirement

THERE IS A DRIVE ON in Rappahannock County to rid the county of old, junked, and abandoned cars. The project is state supported and promoted. Basically, it provides for a payment of fifty dollars per car that is collected. The formula for distributing the fifty dollars is flexible. Ten dollars goes to the county. This provision could be a source of considerable revenue for the county, as the number of visible cars, or parts of cars, in various stages of neglect or abandonment is considerable. If it is assumed that the cars not visible from the road outnumber those within range of vision by seven to one, as the estimated ratio of ice not seen is to that which is visible in iceberg sighting, old cars and hulks could for several years be a major crop in the county. Yet the response to the new program has been limited.

Rappahannock County does not give up its houses, its machinery, its customs easily.

Many houses still in use are over two hundred years old. Some parts of houses, especially chimneys, are of like age. Houses once abandoned, as a rule, are not torn down, at least by older residents. They are left, on the possibility that they may be used again, and if that re-use is not likely, as a reminder to those who survive of the passage, by death or abandonment, of the last residents in the houses. Chimneys are left standing long after all vestiges of houses they once served have disappeared.

The site of old mills is marked by crumbling walls, evidence of dams and of mill ponds and mill races. Mills of later vintage, many of them, still stand, some converted into houses, some into antique and craft shops, some just waiting. Silos stand alone in fields and farm yards, the barns they complemented fallen into decay, or torn down and moved. Some churches have survived loss of faith or of faithful; a few are changed to houses or to shops, and some stand in window-boarded vigil over grass-grown cemeteries. Old filling stations and banks closed during the depression remain, reborn to new purposes and life as antique stores.

Old farm machinery stands in farm yards or in meadows; the most prominent and most numerous among them, the first significant aid to hay makers, the horse-drawn dump rake. Abandoned, or kept in reserve, on suspicion that newer rakes and bailers may break down, the old rakes seem to attract a protective growth of burning nettles.

But the automobile outmatches all other things, houses, churches, machinery, in survivability. The poet Philip Booth, in a poem entitled "Maine," has declared that "when old cars get retired they go to Maine." He then describes them, some as being like cows grazing quietly behind old barns. Others sit in place with backends jacked up, the wheels replaced by pulley or circular saw to grind feed or cut wood. Engine blocks from some are dropped in the Atlantic to serve as anchors for buoys and boats at rest.

Not all old cars go to Maine. Many go to Rappahannock. What few new cars come here may well stay until dismantled or abandoned. Most cars start life in the county as used cars, bought new first in other places. There is no new car sales outlet in the county. There are used car sales lots, and lots with dismantled cars and parts for sale, as well as the scattered remains, the object of the state and county search and solicitation. Some, the still favored ones on blocks, stand in sheds and barns. Some, abandoned when houses were abandoned, crouch in growths of brambles, or in locust thickets. Others hide under cover of honeysuckle or kudzu. Engines under repair, or despaired of, hang from tripods or branches of oak or maple, draining or drained, like deer hung out to cure or butchered hogs, to cool.

It is anticipated that the state and county project may well fall short of the measure of success hoped for by those who conceived it.

Windchill in the County

Keep Your Clothes On

A PROPOSAL TO SELL THE U.S. WEATHER BUREAU, announced near the beginning of the Reagan administration, seems to have been lost forever. Possibly no private companies, or practitioners of weather predictions, such as Willard Scott nationally or Bob Ryan locally, fearing malpractice suits, made any offers to buy. Insurance charges may have been too high.

In any event the reasons given for the proposed sale were never very clear. If reducing the national debt had been the objective, it would have been better to offer for sale more profitable properties, such as radio and television licenses. The right to graze on the public "mind" and "will" could have been granted to the highest bidder in somewhat the same way that the rights to graze sheep and cattle on public lands are distributed.

Although the administration spokesperson, who made the announcement of the proposed sale, did not say so, it was generally assumed that the administration thought that the private sector could give us better weather or more of it, for less money; that weather analysis and predicting might become more competitive and consequently, according to the general belief of the administration that the private sector can always do better than the public one, we might not only get better weather but more accurate predictions as well.

The whole matter received little serious or prolonged consideration at the country store. Predicting the weather in Rappahannock County has long been suspect.

Rappahannock County usually gets more rain and snow than is predicted for the general area. Wind forces, however, are moderated by the protection given by the Blue Ridge Mountains. The county is usually neither as hot nor as cold as its adjacent counties, or weather centers. Because of the uncertainties, persons living here have come to rely on local students of weather, both for long term predictions and for short term ones. Some experts use old German and Swiss forecasting devices, in which the approach of bad weather is indicated by the appearance at the door of the weather house of a scolding woman armed with a broom, and approach of continuing good weather, by a jovial, satisfied man. Protest against this evidence of sexual discrimination has been limited, and may well remain so, if the local weather forecasts maintain a minimal level of superiority over those made more scientifically, or by a balanced crew of male and female predictors.

County weather experts have also held out against the Centigrade measure of temperature. They have stuck with Fahrenheit.

Predictions of rainfall here are made in simple measurements of inches, or parts of an inch. No one gives any attention to 20 percent chance of rain, or any such relative measurements. Heavy snow, here, is distinguished from light snow on the basis of moisture content. The measure of depth of snow is estimated in inches. Windchill reports are not taken seriously, since few persons will take the time to apply the formula, which requires one to take off his or her clothes, then take the wind velocity and multiply it by one and a half, and then subtract this figure from the temperature, if the temperature is above zero, and add it if the temperature is below zero (or both add and subtract if the process carries one's calculations past the zero point).

The discomfort index, a mathematical combination of temperature and humidity readings applicable to government employees in Washington working in non-airconditioned buildings and triggering their early release, is not recognized in the county.

Generally the forecasts of local weather are tested against the *Farmer's Almanac* as the best source of weather information for Rappahannock County.

Trash

Route 618 Subject to Scientific Study

IN RECENT YEARS the three-mile stretch of Route 618, from the site of the old Land's Mill to the Hazel River was possibly the best kept, litter-free stretch of road in Virginia. This was not due to the thoroughness of the highway department, but almost exclusively, because of the care and attention given to the road and roadside by Hoppy Hopkins, a retired or semi-retired professor, and his wife Jane.

Following Hoppy's death both the litter along the road and the increase in the groundhog population in the area testify to his absence, for along with his concern over litter, Hoppy was an unrelenting groundhog hunter.

I and others who live along the road have taken note of the slowly accumulating litter, and out of concern for the beauty of the road, and because of guilt over having neglected a duty which we had come to leave to Hoppy and to his wife Jane, we even began to talk about doing something about the situation. First we postponed our undertaking until summertime, waiting, we said, for the honeysuckle to recede and then for the poison ivy to die.

Meanwhile I conducted an objective, socio-psychological survey of the litter along the way, in the manner in which I thought Hoppy would have wanted us to study the matter.

First, I noted that the traffic on the road was a controlled factor. Traffic is relatively light, the vehicles generally driven by persons who know where they are and where they are going. Occasionally a lost driver may get on the road, but as a rule there are few transient motorists. The vehicles I noted seem to be about standard mix, except for a more than average percentage of pickup trucks, during the hunting season.

In our first study, I acknowledged that we did not have comparative figures, and therefore could not discover or report trends. I recognized also that some of the litter items undoubtedly are still concealed by honeysuckle, poison ivy, ferns, and other plant growth, and that later figures, adjusted, will be more accurate.

I submit my findings as within the range of about a four percent margin of error, which seems to be the standard for error in television network political projections.

I found as my first significant observation that there was a full range of drink container litter from one brandy bottle to one milk carton. The heaviest concentrations, or highest numbers of litter items, were beer bottles and cans and similar containers for sugar loaded drinks.

By a clear margin, the major litterer was the Budweiser beer drinker, casting both bottles and cans at the roadside. Not only did the Bud containers outnumber any other single brand of cast-off containers, but they outnumbered all other beers put together, including Michelob, Old Milwaukee, Pilsner, Red White and Blue, and Schlitz, Pabst, and single entries of Coors, and a beer called Goebel. Budweiser might well add a line to its commercial, urging its drinkers not to litter, in their happiness.

Among the soft drink cans counted along the road, the difference was not quite as marked as it is among beer cans. Mountain Dew led all the rest by a considerable margin, that is one on one, but not in overall totals. Pepsi Cola and Coca Cola ranked in a tie for second, followed by Dr. Pepper,

Seven Up, and then Tab and Diet Pepsi, and one abandoned container that once held some kind of grape drink. The significant conclusion from this data is that Mountain Dew drinkers are different, and that those who drink sugared drinks seem more ready to litter than those who are into diet drinks.

The data on solid food litter and containers for non-liquids was more difficult to gather. Zagnut candy wrappers and bags that once held cheese popcorn, along with plastic cups, were most numerous. In statistically insignificant numbers I noted also several potato chip bags, a cupcake mold, and one Milky Way (the candy of the Olympics) wrapper.

According to my estimates, if the standard $50 littering fine could have been assessed for each violation in this three-mile stretch of road, the state could have collected some $5,000!

Listening

Rand Corporation Method

THE RAND CORPORATION, one of America's leading corporations, which also features a think tank, has for some time been running an advertisement in the better business magazines touting a course in "Listening." The advertisement suggests, if it does not positively assert, that most persons, or many, fail to rise in the business world and in the professions because they do not listen, or do not listen correctly.

I did not subscribe to Rand Corporation's course, but was moved by its advertisements to wonder whether I was listening well. Possibly, I thought, I had been missing something or many things. Possibly I was not thinking clearly because I had not been listening.

I resolved to listen attentively for a whole day, beginning just before dawn when I listened to the varied notes of the small birds, wood sparrows, principally, I think, in the cedar hedge adjacent to my bedroom window. After a half hour of this listening, I heard the first morning cawing of the crows, followed by the cry of the catbirds, and of the blue jays, and then the drumming of woodpeckers on dead pine and tulip trees. By seven o'clock, when I should have been getting up to begin work on a book I am supposed to be writing, I was still in bed, listening. New sounds had come on, domestic ones: the crowing of Mary McCoy's rooster and the bleating of her goats. The early morning plaintive mooing of Bill Senkewitz's cow, either calling for a calf, or for a neighbor's bull. Then came the raucous sound of Nelson Lane's jackass, reminding me of dawn in Jerusalem, and prompting me to listen in vain for the cry of muezzin, calling the faithful to morning prayer.

All through the day, I kept listening, according to the prescription of Rand Corporation. Each time, as I was about to stop listening and go in to my typewriter, another sound distracted me: the mid-morning scream of a hawk, the skittering sound of the kingfisher as he skimmed above the pond water, the September hummingbird, buzzing in late flowers, the noon-day yelp of wild turkeys. I did interrupt my listening for lunch, but still unsatisfied and apprehensive that, if I left off my listening, I might spoil the whole Rand Corporation scheme.

I returned to listening in the afternoon resting in a lawn chair. I noted the changing sound of the wind as it first came over the mountain, moving the high pines and oaks and tulip trees that marked the ridge, and then worked down to gentler leaves of hickory and ash and to the almost soundless movement of the birch leaves and of the weeping willows. When no wind blew, I could hear the maple leaves ticking onto the ground, counting off the end of summer.

During my afternoon walk, I continued to listen, to the sound of squirrels and chipmunks among the leaves and of rabbits, to the grunting to John Glasker's pig loose in the woods, unless it was the resident bear I heard. I noted the changing sound of Beaver Dam Creek as more water fed into it on its run down to the old mill site. I noted also, in Thoreau fashion, the sound of the jets overhead, and of trucks on distant Route 552, as well as a muffled rumble of thunder beyond the mountains.

Late afternoon brought on the bobwhite and the mockingbirds, and at dusk the sad singing of coon hounds waiting for night. Then, as darkness settled in, the bass notes of the bullfrogs followed and the shrill scrapings of the cicadas, the hooting of the owls, again the lonely bellowing of cattle and the jackass once more.

I had listened all day, and had come to none of the clear insights and understandings Rand Corporation had all but promised. Nor had I touched pen or typewriter.

PERSONAL & OTHER AFFAIRS

Cold Comfort

Building Character in the Country

A BIOGRAPHICAL SKETCH I once read of Archbishop Weakland of Milwaukee made a special point of the fact that the Archbishop, as a small boy, lived in a house in which the bedrooms were unheated, and that on cold mornings he would go downstairs in his night clothes to change in the heat that radiated from a central coal stove. This experience, among others, had, according to the article, formed the Archbishop's positive character. The report reminded me that I had had the same experience, in the same kind of house, but I had been unaware of its character-building potential. I recall that it was rather pleasant, even exciting, to change clothes, close to the coal stove in the living room, watching the flames through the stove's isinglass windows, a pleasure which was lost when what we called "city water" was put in the town and a furnace and hot water heating system installed in our family house. The new heating arrangement was called "central heating," a misnomer, I think, since it was not central heat but distributed heat with radiators in every room. The old system, if it can be called a system, was truly central, and not much more than that. In any case, central or not, I was exposed to the character building of the cold bedroom and the hot stove during my formative years, and may have, without my knowing it, benefited from the experience.

The report of the Archbishop's hardship and character building moved me to recall other reports of character-building experiences which may have affected my character. For example, in the presidential campaign of 1972 it was noted that Senator Muskie, one of the candidates, had as a boy taken Saturday night baths in a wash tub set on the kitchen floor. This information was not presented as incidental information but as having bearing on Mr. Muskie's presidential qualifications. I had had the same treatment but had never associated anything in my character with that fact. My brother and I had bathed in the same way, again before we got the city water and the furnace and a bathroom complete with tub. The water we used was cistern water, moderately warm as it came from the reservoir on the cook stove, with an extra shot of boiling water from the tea kettle added. As I remember we enjoyed the baths, more than later ones in proper bathtubs. We were repeatedly warned against splashing water on the kitchen floor. This restraint may have been character building.

Then in 1975, I discovered that I had either missed a chance to build my character or that my character had been built in some measure without my knowing of it. In that year *Newsweek* magazine, in a full page advertisement, set out what they considered both the negative and the positive attributes of Jimmy Carter as a potential president of the United States. Among the positive ones was listed the fact that Jimmy as a boy had used, down in Georgia, an outdoor toilet. I had that same experience but had never thought to take any public credit for it. In fact I had had the experience under conditions more taxing and demanding than the conditions in Georgia. In Minnesota there was the summer exposure to bumblebees and outhouse wasps, which I assume was also the case in Georgia. But the winter exposure in Minnesota, in twenty-below-zero weather, must have been an even stronger force for developing courage and fortitude than any exposure in Georgia.

I might add a fourth and possibly more powerful character-building experience than those of the Archbishop's, Senator Muskie's, and Jimmy Carter's. My test is cleaning out a chicken house after the first spring thaw, following a long, frozen winter.

Many residents of Rappahannock County have had their characters formed through such tests and trials. Some still are being tried, tested, and proved.

Promise of Springtime

Optimism from Jehovah's Witness

AFTER AN ABSENCE of nearly two weeks I returned to Rappahannock County on a Friday early in May. I was apprehensive that I might well have missed the best part of May. I found that I had missed some things. The apple blossoms evidently had come and gone while I was absent, for the apple trees were now in green leaf. There was no sign of redbud at wood's edge, or of wild cherry. The dogwood was still in bloom, however. Golden ragweed was thick in the pastures, and so were the buttercups.

I found the wild azaleas blooming where they should have been, along Route 618. The grass in the pasture was as high as the knees of the cows, and the hay in the meadow was ready for cutting. Goat's-beard and wild phlox, and sweet cicely and poppies bloomed at roadside. A few May apple blossoms still clung to the stems beneath the umbrella leaves. So, encouraged, I bought tomato plants at Burke's store when I went to the post office on Saturday morning to pick up my mail.

On returning home I decided to check through the mail before planting the tomatoes. I was in for a shock. There was no spring-like optimism, not even hope, in my mail. Evidently the prophets of gloom, the managers of direct mail programs, know not how the seasons run.

Mayapple

First I opened a letter from *The American Sentinel,* warning me that American children are being brainwashed and that unless the process is stopped, and our nuclear arms build-up continued, we and the children may eventually be destroyed by Soviet nuclear arms. Offsetting this letter was another, from the Community for Creative Non-Violence, suggesting that the only way we can escape nuclear destruction is to stop building nuclear arms.

I received an appeal, endorsed by Katherine Hepburn, asking for support for population control, in some form or other, and restating the Malthusian theory that the world would be destroyed by excessive numbers of people. Countering this appeal was one from The Right to Life organization, asserting that population control, in some forms, would destroy civilization. The choices were not easy.

There was a letter from a Republican Committee asking for help in electing a Republican president and making predictions of dire things to come if a Republican were not chosen. Discounting or offsetting that letter was one from the Democratic National Committee informing me that the chairman of that party thinks I will agree with him that the election of a Republican president might well be disastrous for the nation.

There was an appeal, over the signature of James Watt, the former Secretary of the Interior, asking for help and saying that President Reagan had been a voice "in the wilderness." Critics of the President, I recalled, had been charging that Reagan wanted to destroy the wilderness. Why, I wondered, was he "crying" there. The Secretary, in any case, in biblical spirit, wanted help in subduing the wilderness. His appeal was balanced, or countered, by a letter from the *National Geographic Magazine,* urging me to buy a book entitled *"Our Threatened Inheritance",* so that I would know what that inheritance is, how it is threatened, and what to do about the threat. There seemed no middle ground, or wilderness.

There was an appeal from the American Heart Association asking for contributions in support of research in heart disease, a good cause. There was no clear counter appeal to this, or to appeals for help in cancer care and study. There was instead a distracting lead article, in a pamphlet called "Executive Health," "On That Treacherous Gland, Your Prostate."

I was becoming depressed, near despair. There seemed no way out, all escapes were blocked.

I decided that I had had all of the warnings and admonitions I could stand, and was about to throw the rest of my mail, unopened, into the waste basket, when I was distracted by the barking of my dog. When I went out to investigate, I found that a large, green Cadillac, of some years' service, had been driven into my driveway. I thought that it might be a bottle gas salesman, or possibly someone intent on selling me a Culligan water-softener system. It was neither. It was a Jehovah's Witness, who had come over the mountain from Luray, in Page County, Virginia, to warn the people of Rappahannock County of the signs and portents of the destruction of the world and the coming of the Kingdom.

I listened to his message, to his quotations from the Bible, the promise of Armageddon, with rising optimism. I told him

133

that after the depressing mail I had just been reading, that his words had uplifted my spirit. I bought three pamphlets from him and after he had gone, planted my tomatoes in trust that I might get one more crop before the end.

The Heart Has a Way of Its Own

A HEART ATTACK is not a pleasant experience although each one is, I believe, unique.

Heart attacks are supposed to be meaningful. Norman Cousins has written a book about his. I have not yet found the meaning of mine. I have experienced no unusual perceptions or special insights or inspiration as yet. I may need more time, since the attack took me somewhat by surprise. The statistics and general indicators of potentiality for attack, other than that I am a male and am getting older, were reassuring. I had low blood pressure, a slow pulse, had never smoked, and had no family history to worry about, and was only slightly overweight and under exercised. I was suffering or enduring only the normal stress of the politics of the Reagan Administration with some carry forward from the Carter Administration.

It was not that I was unaware of what the immediate signs of a heart attack are. From reports of friends who had had experience, and from warnings and admonitions from the media, I was alert for the pain in the left arm, shortness of breath, and sharp pains in the chest. None of these warnings was given me.

My advice to all is not to rely on statistical assurances or wait for identifiable symptoms. If you have sensations, painful or marginally so, in the heart's region of your chest, that are different from any that you have ever experienced, call for help right away. In my case the calls began about 2 a.m., Labor Day: to a neighbor who knew the name of a doctor to call in Culpeper; another call to the doctor, who said he would be waiting; then to a neighbor, closer than the rescue squad, to drive me to the hospital, some twenty-five minutes away.

The doctor and his staff were waiting and ready as promised - Dr. Al Cramer, who advised me on arrival that he was also the State Chairman of the Republican party of Virginia. This was a confidence builder.

In any case, all went well. I am on the way to recovery, I am told, after such various processes as echograms and angiograms. I am promised a good life and even some things, according to a reassuring pamphlet, that I have never done successfully before such as ballroom dancing and golf. My last score for eighteen holes, made some fifteen years ago, was ninety-six. I am also advised by the pamphlet that I am ready for light housekeeping, including window washing, but am temporarily banned from heavy vacuum cleaning, a prohibition I will surely honor.

As of now I have come to only two sure conclusions. The first is that a person should have a special and detached respect for his or her heart, possibly address it as Mr. Heart, or as Ms. Heart, and not be very certain of it or possessive, or address it familiarly as one might kidneys or liver as "my kidneys" or "my liver."

The heart has a way of its own, pumping away, on its own time and schedule, generally reliable and regular and uncomplaining; but it demands respect.

My second clear conclusion is that one should not eat barbecued spare ribs on the evening of a heart attack, even if barbecued by that master of the open grill, Thomas Geoghegan.

Meanwhile I am reading the cards I have received from friends and enemies, and have begun reading the books sent to me: seven about Ireland (one of them of Irish love stories, generally depressing); a biography of Dwight Eisenhower; a history of the *Washington Post* (critical, which increased my enjoyment); a history of Civil War Battles of 1864; one on the Atlantic coastal areas; and one on the ends of the earth - the Arctic Eskimo lands, Siberia, the Congo, and outer Manchuria.

Old Sperryville Bookshop

A Therapeutic Dog

A RECENT *NEW YORK TIMES* ARTICLE, after stating that many people in this country keep dogs, cats, birds, fish, and other pets, and that most people like the pets they keep and know, more or less, why they do, makes the further statement that the non-human companions can help improve the mental and physical health of their keepers and even extend their lives, something the Times writer, Jane E. Brody, says the pet keepers might not realize.

Her article is bolstered by scientific research at a number of universities. The Andrus Gerontology Center at the University of Southern California, for example, reports that pets, especially dogs, can offer protection, companionship, and unconditional love, all of which may contribute to a more contented and longer life for their owners. Studies of the pet-human relationship at the University of Minnesota, Pennsylvania State University, and Ohio State College of Medicine have made similar findings.

Since I have a dog that I am fond of, treat well, and boast of whenever I can, usually to persons who have never met the dog, I was moved to pursue the article to discover the secret of our relationship: its reciprocal character; what traits of character in the dog might have made my life more tranquil than it might otherwise have been; and, since I had just had a heart attack, what I might expect from the dog to ease and hasten my recovery and possibly even contribute to my longevity. In other words, to discover, if I could, the "therapeutic value" of my dog.

I was struck by the first observation in the report from the Southern California Gerontology Center: pets are "non-threatening, non-judgmental, open, welcoming, accepting, and attentive." My dog is all of these, but not predictably so. She has not yet bit the hand that feeds her, but she has snapped at the hand that tries to comb or brush her hair, cut her toenails, or put flea spray on her. She has nipped at guests who shuffle their feet under the dining room table or cross their legs in the living room, and has done the same to persons who surprise her by sudden gestures or high-pitched laughter. She has not, I must acknowledge, ever gone to the extremes of Lance, the dog of Shakespearean fame, who did worse things both under the table and out from under it.

Sometimes she is open and welcoming, extremely so. Other times she will not get off a bed or out from under a table to greet me at the door. She is clearly judgmental and will reject a Rolaids but readily accept a Tums. Some days she is attentive and likes to be petted; other days she seems to be deaf and wholly unresponsive.

The USC study notes that dogs do not talk back. My dog has not yet talked back. I have talked to her, a live dog, hoping that I might get some response. Since McKenzie King, former Prime Minister of Canada and for a long time a respected world statesman, reported in his diaries that he talked to his dead dog and was answered, I was hopeful.

One or more of the dog/pet-human studies have found that pets help to organize a person's day. A dog, for example, will in the name of regularity insist on your getting up at, say, 7:00 AM, to be walked or let out or fed. Not so with my dog. She resents being stirred for her morning exercises, unless there is some special excitement outdoors, before nine o'clock. And if she had her way, she would have everyone in bed by 8:00 PM, which, after patiently waiting out the evening meal and with a disdainful glance at the television set, is about the time she stalks off to the bedroom.

Dogs especially, according to two European studies also cited by *The New York Times,* can make friends for their owners in Hyde Park and on the streets of Oslo. I am hard pressed to recall any friendship that I have made through my dog's meeting other dogs on city streets. The sight of another dog on a leash seems to stir her basic herding instinct and move her to some vague conclusion that the dog leashee, or whatever the creature at the other end of the strap should be called, is in need of help. She is moved to this reaction especially by poodles, Afghans, and long-haired terriers of all kinds. It is certain that the pet owners and walkers make few friends among the people whose flower beds, ivy, lawns, and curbs mark the line of the morning and evening exercise routes.

She can, after an encounter with an electric fence and some association of that with lightning and crackling fires, anticipate a thunderstorm better than most weather persons and give advance warning of it by trembling and seeking the shelter of a hall closet. I have been forced to choose between the comfort and reassurance of my dog or a wood fire in my fireplace on winter nights. She is subject to some kind of allergy to smoke and also, being of Australian ancestry, seems to shed as winter approaches and to grow a heavier coat for the summer.

Despite all of her characteristics which run counter to those considered as desirable and as contributing to quiet, contentment, and possibly to a longer life, I have concluded that my dog is a therapeutic dog, but in a very subtle and negative way. She does not for long let me dwell on my own troubles.

Play and Work

THE PHILOSOPHER-HISTORIAN'S observation that "Art imitates life" has long been accepted. Now it appears that leisure imitates work, not just in its pleasant satisfaction but also in troubles and pain.

While OSHA, the Occupational Safety and Health Agency of the federal government, labors early and late, manfully and womanfully, to protect workers from dangers to health and safety in factories and other work areas, ranging from black lung and asbestos poisoning to toilet seats, ladders, and mop pails, pain-causing and disabling afflictions multiply in the world of leisure, play, and also in the arts.

One of the most publicized of the leisure sports-induced ailments is "tennis elbow," the treatment of which has become a growth industry for specialists in orthopedics. In the past, physical disorders resulting from excessive sports activities were kept more or less secret for fear of ridicule and public disfavor. Such disorders, some at least, have taken on social significance and become marks of status for those afflicted, as the Hapsburg jaw distinguished that family for centuries and gout was accepted as a mark of membership in upper class British society in the 18th and 19th centuries.

The common counterpart of "tennis elbow" has long been known in work rooms of the needle trades and along assembly lines.

Surfer's knots, the distinguishing lumps on ankles and shins caused by kneeling on surf boards, affect fewer persons than does the tennis elbow. Surfer's knots are more exclusive, but basically of the same nature as afflictions suffered by persons who pursue or perform ordinary labors. Roughly comparable to surfer's knots, says Dr. Sudhaker Rao of Henry Ford Hospital in Detroit, is "ladder shins," found in painters, window washers, and persons who install automatic garage doors. The latter disability resembles in some respects such long recognized work-related disorders as "housemaid's knee," "bargeman's bottom," and "bartender's elbow."

Disorders in body functions resulting from gambling and from playing modern electronic and other games have grown in numbers and severity to the point that they too are receiving medical attention. The leading study thus far publicized is one by Dr. Gary Myerson of Atlanta's Emory University. The disability has been given a name "Arcade Arthritis," a condition which manifests itself principally in inflamed tendons in arms and hands. Dr. Myerson reports that he does not consider video games as inherently dangerous. He does not recommend football or baseball as alternatives for most persons.

"Cuber's Thumb", a swelling of the thumb resulting from prolonged manipulation of the Rubik cube, has also received medical recognition.

Gamblers and those who assist them are always showing signs of occupation - and recreation - caused disintegration. A podiatrist reports that foot problems among workers and gamblers at Atlantic City casinos (he notes that the same is true in Reno and in Las Vegas) are reaching "epidemic proportions." The expert in this field of medicine and health is Dr. Leonard Hymes of Pleasantville, New Jersey.

According to the doctor, this foot condition known as "casino feet" is now recognized as a "status symbol" in the gambling fraternity. Dentists, barbers, hairdressers, and bank tellers suffer from the same affliction but in their case, since the condition is one that arises from occupational activities within the range of authority of OSHA, it does not merit status recognition for them.

More serious in their implications for culture are two afflictions, actually occupational hazards for some persons, reported recently in medical journals. One affects flute players. Labeled "flutist's neuropathy," it is marked by numbness of the left index finger and is considered a minor threat to chamber music. The other is called "Gamba leg." The first case of "Gamba leg" to be clearly identified, diagnosed, and named was that of a woman musician whose upper left leg fell asleep as she practiced on a stringed instrument known as the Viola Da Gamba, a close musical relative of the cello. The medical expert on this subject is one Dr. Philip Howard, who wrote of it in a recent *New England Journal of Medicine.* Dr. Howard's report does not say whether the condition is one that occurs only in female Viola Da Gamba players or why it affects only the left leg. Further study may be required, but the disability seems to be very much like a similar disability suffered by milkmaids in the pre-milking machine days when they worked from a one, two, or three legged stool, holding the milk pail between their knees.

Taken all together, these reports clearly indicate that medical research has not become hidebound or narrow and restricted in its scope. They at least suggest that the criticism of doctors begun by W. C. Fields decades ago - when in one of his movies, he fell off a circus wagon and, as he lay on the ground in evident pain, cried out in his agony, "It's Wednesday; take me to a golf course. I need a doctor." - is not justified.

The Free Lunch Under Fire

THE FREE LUNCH has been under fire off and on in recent times from politicians, economists and moralists. It has become the sign of unrealistic hopes and beliefs, of unsound economic theory, of moral turpitude and social disintegration.

Governor Brown of California, an existential politician, once denied its existence. "There is no 'free lunch,'" he said. Not at noon or at any other time. And that is that, is that, is.

Former presidential adviser Walter Heller, as an economist, is necessarily a relativist. (It is said that when one inquires as to the state of Walter's health, he gives a seasonally adjusted report.) In any case, in defense of his reputation and record as an economist, Mr. Heller used the concept of the "free lunch" as a means of ridiculing politicians and economists who used the 1964 tax cuts recommended by economist Heller to justify the tax cuts they proposed in 1978. "Sound the trumpet and hear the herald," wrote economist Heller. "There is, after all, such a thing as a free lunch. And it's not soft-headed liberals but hard-headed conservatives that bear the glad tidings."

One attack on the free lunch, led by President Carter, was based on equity and morality. The President's special target was the "three-martini lunch." He was also opposed to a free or tax-deductible "no martini lunch," a one-martini lunch, a two-martini lunch, and whatever lay beyond the three-martini lunch, when the count is usually lost, or highly confused.

The critical point for the President was between the second and third martini. There were some experts, on both martinis and tax deductibility, who said that this was a little late in the lunch to draw the line. They felt that the breaking point should come somewhere between the end of the first martini and the end of the second. These same experts generally held that the cost of the first martini should not be deductible, on the grounds that it creates no good will. Deductibility, they said, should come into play as the lunch proceeds through the second and third martinis.

Meanwhile the Internal Revenue Service moved on corporate luncheons; the White House began charging members of the congressional leadership for the breakfasts they have with the President; and the Supreme Court held that the value of noon lunches given to state troopers must be included in their income for tax purposes.

As yet untouched by the subtle reach of the President, the IRS, and the courts is the "free lunch at noon," an institution as old as the farm auction. It traditionally was offered during the break between the morning sale of cattle and the afternoon sale of machinery, tools and household goods. It consisted, as a rule, of ham sandwiches, made with home-cured ham and store-bought bread, and coffee that was always either too hot or too cold, served in tin cups supplied by the auctioneer. (I had an uncle who was an auctioneer. He kept his tin cups in two gunny sacks in the back seat of his car. As he drove, there came from the sacks a gentle sound of tin on tin, somewhat like the sound of distant Chinese bells.) It was standard practice to provide two kinds of cake at the lunch - one chocolate and one white or yellow - until marble cake, which combined both, was invented.

In more settled rural areas, the lunch at noon is already threatened by the mobile canteens, which provide sandwiches untouched by human hands, wrapped in cellophane, and serve coffee in insulated plastic containers. This non-free lunch meets the new standard of accountability.

But there are still secret places in the back country where "the free lunch at noon" lives on, safe from the IRS, the FDA, the White House, and the mobile canteen.

Rappahannock Boots

IN READING a pre-Christmas catalog from one of the better known sportswear suppliers, also one of the most expensive, operating out of Freeport, Maine, my eye fell on a boot that looked very much like a pair I own. In fact I have owned and worn this pair for nearly six years, on and off, summer and winter, rain or shine, snow or mud, or Rappahannock County dust and clay.

I bought my boots in the country store in Amissville. After six years they were beginning, not to show wear, but more like feel wear. There was no particular, marked weakness showing. The leather upper seemed a little stiffer than usual, even after a treatment of mink grease. There were signs of cracking although no cracks where uppers joined soles. The inside liners felt thin in a few spots, not quite covering the clinched nail heads, as though the boots were wearing out from the inside at about the same rate they might be wearing out from the outside, or better, wearing in, or apart. Both heels were down a little, and whereas I could not discern that the soles were at any one point growing thin, I have occasionally felt small stones through the soles recently, something I cannot recall in earlier years.

All of these scattered and slight reminders of the changing conditions of my boots and of the passage of time, moved me to give a second look at the catalog boot, and later, for comparison, at the Red Wing Rappahannock boot in the Co-Op store on Route 211. I recall having paid $12.00 for my boots in 1977; even at the Co-Op the price as expected had risen but not to the level of the catalog boot, which was listed at $83.25 postpaid.

The descriptions of the boots, in catalog and on ticket at the store, were almost the same: "Rugged, handsome, for work or casual wear." "Hard wearing full grain cowhide uppers." "Deep-dip toeline for easier foot entry." "Medium Western toe." "Arch-supporting innersole." "Stacked leather heels, with rubber caps, for longer wear." "Molded heel counters." "Pull tabs for easy on and off." The only noticeable differences between the two boots, other than price, were a leather sole on the more expensive one, obviously less useful, and an inner lining of tanned cowhide. I could never understand the need for inner liners, unless one regularly went without socks.

I am sticking with my old boots, for at least one more season, not just for their service to me, which I know about, but out of respect for their reputation. As I have picked up the word from more experienced users, these boots are fully waterproof if enough mink grease is used (even some of the

144

synthetic leather preservers will work). They are also proof against snake fangs, obviously against briars and wildberry thorns, hedge roses and spurs of young locust, and barbed wire. It is claimed that they provide protection too, although it is not to be relied upon too often, against the teeth of errant chain saws, against axes, dog and even hog bites.

I was tempted to buy a second pair to be kept in waiting, but to do so seemed, if not dishonest, at least as indicating lack of faith or loyalty.

I will stay with my boots, as the deacon did with the famous one-horse shay, expecting them to disintegrate, totally, on completing their life's span. Then I will buy another pair, certain that a boot of such merits will survive changing styles, politics, even civilizations.

Christmas Greens and the Mistletoe

RAPPAHANNOCK COUNTY is well supplied with Christmas green-trees, shrubs, and trailing vines.

It has pine trees of various kinds, native as well as some that have been imported, along with spruce and fir. It has hemlock and cedar and holly, tree and bush, and laurel. Magnolias and camellias, which can stand the loss of a branch or two as Christmas offerings. It has ivy and running ground cedar, which my daughter, who has studied biology, says is properly called lycopodium, or wolf foot, and may be a protected species, if not an endangered one. In any case, she warns, one should use it carefully, perhaps to wrap a stair rail, or drape a door, but not wastefully in wreaths.

All of these greens have an accepted place in Christmas today and most of them were accepted in Christmases past, although a few had to be purged of minor pagan identifications and associations before they were accepted into the Christian celebration. Most have gone beyond that acceptance and have become secularized by advertisers.

Holly and ivy were depaganized centuries ago by church action. There remains one Christmas green which still lives without church blessing. It is not common in Rappahannock, but it is present. If one watches carefully and knows what seems out of place or time, and knows what to look for, he may see it in a few places, usually in oak trees, along Route 522 and along Route 231, and along lesser roads of the county. It is mistletoe. I hesitate to call it a plant for it is more of an implant, a parasite.

Mistletoe should not be taken lightly as other Christmas greens and plants. Kissing under the mistletoe may involve risks beyond those ordinarily assumed by those who engage in the practice.

It has a long history in pagan cultures. No one can be sure that it has lost all of those early powers even though there is doubt that it ever had them.

The Druids of Ireland were its chief promoters and made fine distinctions relative to its use. Only mistletoe that had grown in parasitical association with an oak tree had sacred or magical powers. That from poplar, apple, or other trees was suspect, and if it was to be useful, in religious rites, had to be transferred to an oak and draw sustenance from that tree before it could come to possess power.

The mistletoe had to be cut down by a Druid priest using a golden knife and caught in a white cloth before touching the ground.

Its powers, when properly used, were significant. It was called "allheal," and believed to be a cure for mental disorder, especially epilepsy. It was especially effective if used to treat fresh wounds. Modern science has not been able to find any evidence or proof that there is anything in mistletoe that has medical value, which adds to the mystery.

It was also believed to be an aphrodisiac and to have power to make the barren, human and animal, fertile. This power may explain the kissing under the mistletoe which, according to mistletoe experts, does not mean anything unless the sprig of mistletoe has berries and whoever is involved in the osculation picks a berry after the act.

Those who venture to capture mistletoe and bring it in from an oak tree, if they cannot use a golden knife as the Irish Druids did on the sixth of the moon, might try to knock it out of the tree with stones as did the Welsh. Rifle fire might be accepted, but not a shotgun blast.

The Christmas message of the Mistletoe, the Christian one, is that it was a sign of new life, of green, in the barren oak. In more sophisticated explanations, it was also noted that it was life from outside, not from the tree.

Whether one accepts the pagan or the Christian explanation of the mistletoe, the scientific or unscientific reports of its powers, it is not to be trifled with. The careful would do better to kiss under the Christmas tree or under holly leaves.

Uncle's Day

A Force for Family Stability

A NEW YORK TIMES article once proposed the establishment of a national "Aunt's Day" to go along with, or supplement, Mother's Day and Father's Day, and also Grandparents' Day. The *Times's* article made no reference to the latter day, which has been in existence since 1978, when the Congress of the United States, despite its concern over difficult problems of that time, such as energy, inflation, taxes, and "detente," found time to be thoughtful and considerate. The Congress passed a resolution setting up "Grandparents' Day" and set the first Sunday after Labor Day as the date for its observance.

The report on the resolution required, by the rules of the House of Representatives, an inflationary impact statement. At the time of the passage of the resolution it was predicted that establishing the special day would have no such impact. The experience of the years since the passage of the resolution seems to bear out the prediction. There is no objective evidence that the establishment of the special day has had much effect on family relationships, stability, general happiness, or on the economy.

Now Aunt's Day is proposed. I have no particular objection to such an establishment. Aunts have been and still are important in the family structure, but their role remains, certainly in Rappahannock County, what it always has been, primarily supportive, generally of mothers, sometimes of fathers, also of grandparents.

It is the role of the uncle in family functioning that needs attention, revival, and recognition according to the collective judgment of resident uncles in the county. Establishing a "National Uncle's Day," might do much to accomplish this objective.

The decline of the family in America, according to recent, unpublished studies of limited scope in Rappahannock County, is directly traceable to the de-emphasis and discounting of the role of uncles. The uncle was not supportive of parents as were aunts. Uncles were a free force. They were a place of refuge from dominating aunts (for small boys especially). Uncles were not exactly subversive of parental authority, but they were at least a refuge, a source of contrary position and of a second opinion. They were a bridge between family and society, a role not fulfilled by the traditional aunt. Uncles were useful for transmitting the facts of life, when prudish parents hesitated and the birds and bees were not understood. When the uncle prevailed, unrestrained youths were few.

The term "Dutch Uncle," a stern advisor, roughly comparable to the "Irish Aunt," has made its way into the language. But this conception of the uncle's role is at best a limited and inadequate one. Uncles should be stern about one-fourth of the time and understanding and encouraging the other three-fourths of the time.

According to Patrick O'Connor,
"All children should be Japanese.
All women (mothers and wives) Italian.
All grandparents, Jewish.
All men (husbands and fathers), Montenegrin.
All aunts, single, (German, I would say)
And all uncles, Irish."

The essence of unclehood has been best expressed by Margaret Atwood in a poem called "Game After Supper," from which the following is taken:
"I am hiding in the long grass
with my two. . .cousins.

We hear crickets and our own hearts,
close to our ears,
though we giggle, we are afraid.
From the shadows around
the corner of the house
a tall man is coming to find us.
He will be an uncle
if we are lucky."

All of which, as agreed among the sages of the county, adds up to a good case for a "National Uncle's Day."

Under Siege

A Single Man's House

A MAN'S HOUSE, that is, the house of a man living alone, may be his castle, but if he is not on guard, it will not long be his home. The house of a bachelor is almost always under attack, by persons, men and women, acting as men and women always do, according to Aristotle, under some aspect of good.

The attack on the home may come from strangers, or near strangers, or casual visitors, but more often it comes from close friends and from relatives. It may come from males, but more often, according to current cultural attitudes, it will come from women, sisters and daughters especially.

Any and all of these types of persons are prone to make suggestions about a man's home, how it should be decorated, furnished, how it should be run. They may even do things to it, with or without his approval, sometimes when he is watching, sometimes when he is not watching, things they would never think of suggesting or doing to a woman's domicile.

The potential aggressors are no respecters of wealth, or of rank, or of standard of living. They are as likely to direct attacks on a Fifth Avenue apartment, decorated and furnished in the highest and most expensive style, as on the most modest of male living quarters.

The first challenge is usually negative, restrained, and subtle. Sometimes it is preceded or accompanied by an apology. At the higher and more sophisticated levels of existence, it may be no more than an offhand mention of a decorator who would "certainly be challenged" by the architecture of the building, by its internal lighting or its exposure."

In cruder forms, at more common and more modest levels of existence, intervention may come in reference to condition of slipcovers or curtains or, without words, a not-so-surreptitious running of a finger along a windowsill, across a tabletop, a picture frame, or a lamp. This action may be followed by a questioning announcement that one's cleaning person needs another day of work each week.

These negative attacks can usually be ignored without lasting harm to friendship or to family or personal relationships. In some cases they can be accepted, acceded to, without yielding or sacrificing the integrity of one's home.

It is from the positive frontal attacks that the serious threats arise. This aggression against a man's home often begins in seemingly harmless suggestions that new curtains would brighten a room, and an apparent unselfish offer to help in the selection or even to make the selection. The breakthrough, or break-in, may come with a gift of a throw rug or a pillow or two, followed by the suggestion that the room colors do not match the rug or pillow. The lamps in a man's house, too, are easy and early targets of the remodelers or refurnishers. The lamps are especially vulnerable to attack if they are made out of old shell casings, fire extinguisher tanks, baseball bats, used wine bottles, or old cornets.

A man's kitchen is especially vulnerable and attractive as a target for women visitors, many of whom seem to assume that, despite women's liberation of labor and of responsibility, the kitchen in a single man's home is partly, at least, in their jurisdiction.

The intrusive action may take the form of an open takeover of cooking or other food preparation. In its less immediate and aggressive form the intrusion is likely to show in the rearrangement of kitchen cupboards. (Daughters, according to my observations, are most likely to take this action.)

After the rearrangers have been given the run of a kitchen for any length of time, the man of the home is likely to find on going to the cupboard, in trusting Mother Hubbard manner, not a bare cupboard but one changed, changed utterly. He is likely to find dishes where he once kept cooking supplies; cooking supplies where once glasses stood, etc. Cooking utensils are likely to have been moved according to some mysterious logic I do not understand: pot covers gone from the drawer under the stove - a place that seems a perfectly satisfactory repository - to the oven; frying pans removed from the oven and concealed in some secret place. One may find his refrigerator cleaned - rather, cleaned out. Good food that he had been saving for a week or two gone. And then there is the special case of vanilla extract. I have three daughters. Each, I have found, has a different preference for the placement of that cooking aid.

Bathrooms, next to kitchen, are in line of the reformers' fire. Sometimes the interventions are marginally acceptable, as when, for example, they take the form of gifts of matching towels, or a new shower curtain replacing one that was still good but hanging by only three or four clamps. More often the intervention borders on the irresponsible and the insulting, as in the casting away of good soap remnants, or in the obvious, evidence-leaving act of cleaned mirrors, sinks, and medicine cabinets.

The ultimate challenge, possibly confrontation, begins with the suggestion that pictures should be moved, raised or lowered, regrouped, or hung in some other room, possibly to be taken down altogether, given to a church bazaar or to the volunteer firemen's sale, or even thrown away. This move may have been preceded by a gift of picture or pictures or may be followed by such a gift, which the householder, or homeholder, must either put on his walls, or terminate a friendship or relationship of some other order, or live under continuing duress to explain why he had not hung the picture, or what he had done with it. Worse than a gift of a picture is something like a mounted animal head (not likely to be given by a woman) or even a whole stuffed animal. William Manchester, in his early book on John Kennedy, reports how Vice-President Johnson pursued the President, relative to the whereabouts of a deer head he, the Vice-President, had had mounted for the President, until the latter, finally, put it on a wall in the White House.

The first intrusion of this kind probably occurred when a cave lady visited the cave of the first cave man who did the walldrawings in his cave, possibly in anticipation of the cave lady's visit. (Although it is generally assumed without good evidence that the early drawings were done by men, it is not necessarily so. The cave lady may have decorated her own cave.) In any case, the female visitor may very well have suggested to the cave man that he had done his drawings on the wrong wall, or that he had used a wrong color stone, or had not put the drawings in the best light, or that he had drawn them too high on the wall.

Next to a mounted head, giving some person a representation of his sign of the zodiac is most intrusive. He may not be into astrology, or may not like his sign, or the representation of it, a threefold risk. Whereas there is no sure defense against the picture-intrusion invasion, or possibly incursion, there are some evasive and delaying and diversionary techniques that are helpful. I have established themes for certain rooms. If the picture given me does not conform to the room theme, obviously and logically, or at least for the sake of consistency, it cannot be hung in the room. I now have three such rooms. My living room is reserved for Currier and Ives prints or paintings of horses and hounds. My study, the second protected area, is restricted to representations of authors or artists whom I accept. I am now holding the line with Walt Whitman, James Joyce, Cervantes, William Butler Yeats, Sean O'Casey, and Thomas More.

The third room, recently added to the protected list, is my dining room for which, under extreme pressures to hang a gift picture, I declared that the theme was birds, limited to fighting cocks and Audubon drawings and of more or less domestic, or near domestic, game birds like grouse and wild turkeys.

The other rooms of my house, a second study, a hallway and staircase, two bedrooms, a kitchen, and three bathrooms, are still areas of controversy and of compromise.

If the male homeowner has a dog even the dog's rights and privileges and properties may become the subject of abuse. The dog's toys may be found, after the visitor leaves, in a neat pile in a corner of a room or in a hall. A rawhide bone may have been washed, much to the dog's displeasure, the dog dish run through the dishwasher, and even the dog's blanket put into or through a washing machine. I have never seen or heard of these things having been done to a woman's dog or cat, or to their things, by anyone but the possessor of the pet, or with permission. Not so in the case of men's pets.

Carrol Jenkins

Remembering and Remembered

THE DEATH OF CARROL JENKINS of Rappahannock County early in the month of November of 1988 was little noted beyond the limits of the county. Within the county, however, especially in the western part, he is missed. Something, someone, a force of weight, is missing. There seems to be a slight wobble in the axis of the county. Things are not quite as they were. His voice and comments are missing in the country store. His familiar pickup truck not seen on the county roads. It was not that Carrol did anything of particular or great significance for the county, as a country doctor might have done, or a lawyer or a land owner, a clergyman, or a banker. He filled in; he did what needed to be done.

Carrol made his living principally by buying and selling, by trading and bartering - used cars, and especially used pickup trucks, and horses and cattle. The margins of gain in his transactions were usually slight, like those of a Wall Street broker operating in a tight market. He did not take advantage, but dealt largely with others who knew the trade.

His commercial deportment and relationships were almost purely professional. If he had been dealing in England rather than in Rappahannock County, he undoubtedly would have conducted his business in guineas, along with other professional classes, rather than in pounds and pence.

For nearly ten years he "looked after" my house and small piece of land in the county. No bill was ever presented, nor were fees mentioned, unless he had to hire extra help. I tried to anticipate what I owed him, or what I would owe him, usually leaving a check on the garden tractor seat. If I was in arrears he would casually mention what work he had done in recent days or weeks, or trips he had to take to nearby towns for supplies or repairs. So our relationship survived, even flourished. When he said "don't worry" when I was to be gone from my house for a week or more, I didn't worry.

I was never sure of his reading skills, but he spoke well. He knew animal signs and could read the weather and foretell its changes, not just by day or week, but by seasons. Heavy flowering of locust trees meant a good corn crop, for example.

Carrol was a large man, tall and heavy, somewhat too heavy, but his weight added to his dignity. He carried himself straight, upright, in part because of a back injury incurred, according to a local report, when as a younger man, demonstrating his strength (reputed to have been the greatest in the county), he had, in lifting the end of a tractor, injured a disc or two in his lower back. An additional reason for his upright bearing was that he was blind in one eye, the result of his having been hit in the one eye by a shotgun pellet, while driving birds to waiting hunters. The pellet hole still showed, like the pupil hole drilled in ancient statues.

The combination of the bad back and of the partial blindness gave great dignity and balance to his every move. He always held the center in careful balance, while all else revolved around him. He shifted his weight carefully.

What he did best, what will be missed the most, was to remember - the former residents of the county, the old days, the transitions. He had been there when in the '30s the National Park had been established in the Blue Ridge Mountains, when the mountain farms were taken over by the government, the mountain people displaced and moved out of the mountain. He was there in the '70s and '80s when farm consolidations began to occur, and real estate speculators and income-tax farmers bought up small holdings, turning them into cattle operations or simply holding them waiting for increase in land values in a kind of modern enclosure movement. He protested the tearing down of farm buildings, vacant cabins, and houses, and especially of the chimneys and fireplaces. The old places, he held, should be left as "reminders" of who had lived there, at least until there were no persons who cared to remember, or to be reminded.

The Author

EUGENE J. MCCARTHY was born in Watkins, Minnesota in 1916, graduated from St. John's University in Collegeville, Minnesota, in 1935, and a Master of Arts from the University of Minnesota in 1938.

During World War II, he served as a civilian technical assistant in military intelligence for the War Department. He was acting head of the sociology department at the College of St. Thomas in St. Paul when elected to Congress in 1948.

Re-elected four more times, Mr. McCarthy represented Minnesota's 4th District in the House of Representatives for ten years, serving on Post Office & Civil Service, Agriculture, Interior & Insular Affairs, Banking & Currency, and Ways & Means committees.

Elected twice to the U.S. Senate (1959 to 1971), he served on the Finance, Agriculture & Forestry, Public Works committees and the Senate Special Committee on Unemployment Problems; from 1965 to 1969 he served on the Senate Foreign Relations Committee, chairing the special subcommittee on African Affairs.

His run for the presidency in 1968 electrified the nation and forced a national political debate on issues fundamental to the operation of a democracy. In 1976 and 1992 McCarthy again ran for the presidency to bring forward some discussion of these fundamentals, examined in many of his other books which include:

1968: War & Democracy (Lone Oak Press)
America Revisited (Doubleday)
An American Bestiary (Lone Oak Press)
And Time Began (Lone Oak Press)
Challenge of Freedom (Avon)
Colony of the World (Hippocrene)
Complexities & Contraries (Harcourt)(Lone Oak Press, reprint)
Dictionary of American Politics (Macmillan)
Frontiers in American Democracy (World Publishing)
Ground Fog & Night (Harcourt)
Hard Years: Antidotes to Authoritarians (Lone Oak Press)
Liberal Answer to the Conservative Challenge (Macfadden)
Limits of Power (Holt) (Lone Oak Press, reprint)
Memories of a Native Son (Lone Oak Press)
Mr. Raccoon & His Friends (Academy Chicago)
No-Fault Politics (Times Books)
Nonfinancial Economic (Praeger)
Required Reading (Harcourt)
Selected Poems (Lone Oak Press)
Ultimate Tyranny (Harcourt)
Up 'Til Now (Harcourt)
From Rappahannock County (Lone Oak Press)

The Artist

BARBARA S. BOCKMAN, painter, block print maker and quiltmaker, lives in Fairfax, VA and, with her husband and two sons. Since 1972 she has spent many weekends at a family cabin in the mountains of Rappahannock County. The prints she created for The View From Rappahannock reveal the tranquility, beauty and quiet strength of a place only 75 miles from Washington DC but a world away from its hustle-bustle. Bockman's view of Rappahannock comes from myriad sketching trips along county roads and in its villages, on its farms and estates.

She studied painting and art history at The American University, Washington, DC. Her acrylic, watercolor, oil paintings and block prints have been shown since 1958 in the United States and in France and are included in many private and several corporate collections.

The Photographer

JAMES P. GANNON is a former reporter, columnist and editor for The Wall Street Journal and the Des Moines Register, and author of Irish Rebels, Confederate Tigers, a history of the 6th Louisiana Infantry in the Civil War. He and his wife Joan own and operate the Old Sperryville Bookshop in Sperryville, Va., in the heart of Rappahannock County.